WOMAN UP

DISCOVERING YOUR GOD-GIVEN VOICE IN LEADERSHIP, RELATIONSHIPS, AND CALLING

lori champion

Woman Up
© 2020 by Lori Champion

Published by Insight International, Inc.
contact@freshword.com
www.freshword.com
918-493-1718

ISBN: 978-1-943361-67-0
E-book ISBN: 978-1-943361-68-7

Library of Congress Control Number: 2019921008

Printed in the United States of America.

ENDORSEMENTS

Woman Up explores the unique and valuable gifts women possess as leaders and how those gifts should be celebrated and used to bring life to every environment, whether home, workplace, church, or community. Lori's personal story, as well as scriptural and practical solutions, will empower you to lead at the next level!

—John Bevere
Best-Selling Author and Minister
Co-Founder, Messenger International

Lori Champion has been a champion of women in leadership for over thirty years. She has an incredible ability to lead alongside her husband, Joe Champion, with honor and strength. We are living in a time where being a woman in leadership can be so easily misunderstood. Lori's book, *Woman Up,* challenges women to overcome fears, insecurities, and cultural limitations while encouraging them to rise to the places God has called them to lead.

—Lisa Bevere
New York Times Best-Selling Author
Without Rival and *Girls with Swords*

Woman Up is a book for every woman because every woman is a leader. I know Lori's story will equip you with practical tools and encouragement for finding your place as a leader, navigating what it feels like to be the only woman in the room, and knowing how to steward your gifts to impact people for God's Kingdom.

—Christine Caine
Best-Selling Author
Founder, A21 and Propel Women

I have known Pastor Lori Champion for over a decade. When I read her latest book, *Woman Up*, I smiled, because that's the authentic Lori giving herself to others with transparency. You will love her life stories. You will laugh, you will cry, you will want all those you love to read this book. This book is not just for the ladies; it is for men who value the ladies in their lives. I highly recommend Lori and *Woman Up* to you.

—Sam Chand
Leadership Consultant
Author, *Leadership Pain*

This book is a timely resource for every woman who wants to increase her influence. Whether you're in a work, home, or ministry environment, this book will encourage and empower you to become who God intended you to be. If you're wanting to find your purpose and make a lasting difference, Lori Champion's personal journey paired with biblical wisdom will challenge you to Woman Up!

—Craig Groeschel
New York Times Best-Selling Author
Pastor, Life.Church

Lori Champion is one of my favorite people on the planet. She is such a humble, strong, brilliant, and inspiring leader. I am giddy about this book because we are living in a day and age where there is a lot of confusion, hurt, and pain regarding leadership, women, and the church. Through her story, personal examples and scripture, Lori unpacks wisdom that every woman needs to hear. No matter what season you find yourself in, these insights will bring life and freedom to you and your context. And this isn't just about you becoming who God made you to be, this is about the collateral impact on all the women around you: your daughters, granddaughters, and great-granddaughters, your sisters, nieces, and friends, all becoming fully alive to God's original intention! Let's Woman Up!

—Carolyn Haas
Co-Lead Pastor, Substance Church
Minneapolis, MN

Woman Up is a book you won't put down! Lori Champion knows firsthand the blessings and burdens of being a strong, gifted leader. Inspired by the life of Deborah and other godly role models, Lori delivers a timely call-to-action for leaders at every stage of life. This book will liberate so many women to be all that God created them to be.

—Chris Hodges
Senior Pastor, Church of the Highlands
Author, *The Daniel Dilemma* and *What's Next?*

Lori and her husband, Joe, have been friends of Brian and mine for many years. Lori is dynamic in leadership and lives with endearing devotion to Jesus and building His Church. She believes in the potential within every woman; and I know her personal stories, practical teaching, and heartfelt instruction will infuse purpose into the spirit and heart of every reader.

—Bobbie Houston
Co-Global Senior Pastor, Hillsong Church

DeLynn and I have known Lori and Joe for a very long time and there's so much good to say about them, but one of the greatest is the way Lori has carried herself as a leader. We are so excited she has written this book to inspire young women to find their God-given leadership calling and live it out to the fullest. Her story inspires greatness in others.

—Dino Rizzo
Co-Founder, Association of Related Churches

Woman Up is a celebration of the vital ways that God has gifted and equipped women to lead not only in the home, but in the workplace, church, and community. My friend, Lori's book will empower you to see that your voice isn't just unique, but necessary. If the Church really is the representation of Christ to this world, then we need every voice, and that includes yours.

—Greg Surratt
Pastor, Seacoast Church
Mount Pleasant, SC

Have you been looking to grow as a woman in leadership? This book will encourage and challenge you to become who God intended you to be! Lori Champion transparently shares her own leadership journey along with leadership principles from the Bible that will empower you to Woman Up!

—Holly Wagner
　　Founding Pastor, Oasis Church
　　Founder, She Rises
　　Author, *Find Your Brave*

DEDICATION

To my husband, Joe: You were handpicked for me. You are an answer to my parents' and my own prayers, a man who is strong and secure and who has celebrated, cultivated and called forth my strength as a leader. Thank you for always pushing me to my purpose, and for loving and leading me so well. You have my whole heart, forever.

To my sons, Mason, Connor and Jackson: You are all a Mom's dream come true. I'm so proud of the men you have become and how you are pursuing the God-given dreams and callings on your lives. I not only love you all, but you are my favorite people on Earth to be with.

To Caroline, my first daughter-in-law: I could not have customized a better wife for our son, or fit for our family. You are truly a gift to us. You inspire me with your strength and confidence beyond your years, and your ability to make every person you meet feel so special. I love being your second mom.

To my late father, Bill Mason: Thank you for giving me the best example of a husband, father and man of God that a girl could ever have. You empowered me to lead and even after you went to Heaven, your constant encouragement continues to ring in my ears.

To my mother, Paulette Mason Bilderback: You are a model of grace and dignity and you carefully shaped me, beautifying some of the more abrasive edges and showing me how to act like a lady. Thank you for always believing in me and cheering me on.

To my brothers, Paul and Matthew Mason: You were the unfortunate guinea pigs of my early boss-life, yet you still grew up to love me. I could not be more proud of the men you've grown to be and the beautiful legacies you're building in your families!

To Maw-maw and Paw-paw: I hope you're getting a glimpse of this from Heaven's windows. Your words have always called me up, and your examples have led our entire family to love Jesus.

To my late mother-in-law, Mama Sara: I hit the literal "mother-load" when I married your son and got you as a second mom. Thank you for raising a son who celebrates my strength because of the example you gave to him through your life, and for modeling how to raise leaders as a boy-mom!

To Nancy and Mica: You have both been the leading "Deborah's" in my life for decades. So many leadership truths in my life were taught and caught around your kitchen tables. I'm forever grateful for your investments in my life.

To Abby and Celeste: You are two of the purest and strongest women of God that I know, and God has blessed me abundantly to have you in my life and supporting me through this project. Thank you for reading every word, multiple times, and helping me fully express the stories and leadership truths that God has allowed me to steward.

To the Radiant Sisters of Celebration Church: I dedicate this book to you. I want you to know that whatever season you are in, that what you do is nothing compared to who you are. You have God-purpose to fulfill. I pray that the words on these pages will spring into your hearts and inspire you to never settle, but to say "yes" every day to God and His calling on your lives.

CONTENTS

FOREWORD

There is an endless quest for great leadership resources. My organization has trained leaders in every nation. I'm passionate about seeing people tap into their leadership potential, so they can multiply their influence and their God-given callings. And I'm going to tell you that this book, *Woman Up*, excites me. It contains powerful leadership principles for anyone, but it especially dives into the unique strength and value that women bring to the leadership table. Over the years, I've seen more and more women rise to the highest levels of organizational leadership and companies thrive as a result. In my own life, the most incredible voice of empowerment was my own mother's. I believe the greatest leaders in the world were first identified, not by a boss or a mentor, but by a mom. Women have an eye for greatness, often before it's fully developed or noticed by others.

On a recent visit to Austin, Lori shared with me the vision of this book, and that she was taking the life of one of the greatest leaders in all of the Bible, Deborah, and using the Old Testament account as a backdrop for her book. The truths found in this story are so relevant for today. Deborah was a leader ahead of her time, not constrained by the norms of her gender or time, who secured the respect of men and women and even leaders who outranked her. Through her wisdom and battle strategies, a great victory was won. Yet, she didn't take all the credit. The best leaders enlarge the people around them. *Woman Up* isn't about just growing yourself as a leader, but how to have the type of leadership that causes others to rise around you. By courageously exercising her leadership voice, Deborah lifted others up to fulfill their leadership potential and to live a victorious life. I've always said, "Everything rises and falls on leadership." One of the themes of this book is being an "anti-gravity" leader, and Lori explains in depth how great leaders are able to shift altitudes and attitudes even in down-turned environments.

But more than what the content on the pages says, I am delighted about who is saying it. The best leadership advice isn't taught, it's lived. What inspires us best is not what is said or what is written. We are most inspired by the person who has lived it! When the living is good, the teaching gets better. My friend, Lori Champion, has lived it. I've known her and watched her lead for more than a decade. We teach what we know; we reproduce who we are. The fruit of her life is seen in her family, in her church that she co-leads alongside her husband, Joe, and in the people whom she leads outside of the church—business and community leaders who look to her for wisdom and as a model of consistency and strength.

I commend you for taking time to read this book and to grow yourself as a leader. As you dive into the following pages, you will be cheered on and challenged, but by taking these principles to heart, you will be changed for the better. No matter the position or season you're in, women are made to be difference makers, so get ready to Woman Up!

—John C. Maxwell
New York Times Best-Selling Author

ACKNOWLEDGEMENTS

To John Mason and Jeff Dunn. Thank you for consulting and coaching me through this book writing and publishing process. God surrounded me with the very best in you!

To Daniel Gonzales. Thank you for stepping in at the perfect time and designing the cover of this book! You have worn so many hats for so many years, but my favorite is "friend."

LETTER TO MY YOUNGER SELF

I wish someone had told me what is within these pages when I was younger. I had plans for my life that were jolted off the track with circumstances beyond my control. A lot of doubts and fears took root that I spent years digging out. Thinking about this now, I wrote my "younger self" a letter to let me know it was all going to be okay. Here is what I wrote.

Dear Lori,

At twenty-seven, you've embraced adulthood. Lamentations 3:27 (MSG) says, "It's a good thing when you're young to stick it out through the hard times." As a young woman, you've already stuck through quite a few hard things: watching your 45-year-old father die while preaching on a Sunday morning; losing the church your parents founded and that you always thought you'd be a part of; being diagnosed with cancer while pregnant with your first child, then battling through it with treatments, all while working full time and caring for a little one. Oh, and add to that that your two younger brothers moved in with you and Joe to avoid having to move to the mission field when your mom remarried. So, you took on raising teenagers and a newborn at the same time.

You're now in a new assignment as Joe has become senior pastor of a church in the middle of the Louisiana swamps. For the first time in your life, you aren't "working." Yet being a stay-at-home mom is the toughest job you've ever done. You think this is your normal forever—small town living, struggling to make ends meet, and constantly stepping on LEGOs.

You have many leadership contributions you know you could offer, but in your current role—and with the leaders surrounding your husband—your input is neither requested nor appreciated. The few times you've spoken up have been misunderstood, so you'd rather not say anything at all than to have your hand slapped.

But, don't you worry, this is only temporary.

Your husband did not pick someone who backs down or gives up. He picked a leader. There will be a time when he pulls that woman out of early retirement. Her voice is needed. Her wisdom will open his eyes to blind spots, and her gifts will unlock strategies that only a woman can see.

When God said to Adam, "It is not good for man to be alone," He wasn't just talking to Adam; He was talking to all men. You, and every other woman, were made to be a solution. You have a perspective that companies, households, communities and ministries would suffer without. What's at stake if you don't step up? The flourishing of the people and the organizations you were meant to impact through your voice. Your insight, perspective, and compassion are not unsubstantial, but they are vital in importance.

You aren't to manipulate your way into position. That's not God's way. But, as you seek the Lord, serve Him faithfully, and work with all diligence, you will find yourself walking through doors that only He can open. You will have proven yourself able to be trusted with more when you steward the little.

You cannot do this by yourself. No one can. You need to find older sisters and mother types in the faith. Sit yourself under their training, and absorb their instruction. Don't avoid hard conversations—that will keep you comfortable but incompetent. Allow them to shape you and chisel away the rough edges.

Discipline yourself like a soldier because God has a critical mission for you. There will be times when you're exhausted, where you need a break or an adjustment, but don't quit.

Judges 8:4 tells us that Gideon came to the Jordan and crossed over, he and the 300 men who were with him, exhausted yet pursuing.

Keep pursuing! At times, you may look like a hot mess. But you're a hot mess with a message that the world needs to hear. You have a story to tell, girl!

So, enjoy the season you're in now—the one that you feel like you'll be in forever. As is said, "The days are long, but the years are short." Take in every part of the journey, but don't ever settle. You are a miracle, and your life is meant for the miraculous, not the mundane.

That was the message I wanted my 27-year-old self to hear. It's the message I want you to receive, to hold in your heart, to set before you every moment of the day. Keep living! Your life is going to be incredible.

Woman Up!

CHAPTER 1

WOMAN UP

She is energetic and strong, a hard worker.

Proverbs 31:17 (NLT)

"Be the kind of woman who, when your feet hit the floor each morning, causes the devil to say, 'Oh no, she's up.'"

—Unknown

If I heard him say these once, I heard my dad say them a million times. "Lori, you'd argue with a fence post," as well as, "I hope there's a man on this planet for you to marry who you won't steamroll over." With a strong sense of justice and strong opinions, and no filter or patience to wait for the "right moment" (my mom's frequent, gentle admonition), I wore the first frustration-rooted criticism (or truth) as a badge of honor. The one about not finding a husband actually invoked fear, though I'd never let them see it.

That same Dad encouraged me to channel those sometimes out-of-line strengths into leadership qualities and helped me make an abundance of homemade campaign signs on my many runs for student council offices from third grade through high school, finishing strong with the slogan, "Lori Mason, The Choice of the New Generation." It was a play-off of the popular Pepsi ad of the time, and with it, I would win senior class vice president. The only reason I couldn't run for president was because I was also editor-in-chief of the yearbook. The school felt that was too much work to hold both roles, but I managed to juggle in not one, but two extra jobs after school and weekends. I've never been one to like idle time.

In those early days of being a leader in a large New Orleans public school, a strong backbone was put in me. You wouldn't think that my values would be tested in the late 1980's, but taking a stand before the whole student body and teachers in order to say a prayer that mentioned "God" for our graduation ceremony was a defining moment for me. They wanted the prayer to start, "It is our hope that ..." "Don't even say the word, 'prayer' as it may offend our atheist friends," they said. I, probably red-faced, pled my case against political correctness before the term even existed. And later I'd find out that my stand proved to my overly-sheltering parents that I could be trusted to leave home for the college of my choice, which happened to be one of the top party schools of America. In fact, my dad said, "I could send Lori straight into Hell, and she'd stand up for Jesus." Comparing Louisiana State University to Hell was a little dramatic, but I felt the full weight of my father's endorsement and confidence.

Sometimes you don't pick the fight. Rather, the fight comes to you. And when it comes, we have to learn to Woman Up.

BORN BOSSY

In October, 2000, my husband and I planted Celebration Church in Austin, Texas. Prior to starting the church, I had served in various capacities at the three churches in Louisiana where Joe was an associate or senior pastor. Being in full-time ministry is not new to me; far from it. I am a fifth-generation church leader. My father was a pastor.

On both sides of my family, I had grandfathers and great-grandfathers as well as grandmothers and great-grandmothers who were pastors. And my great-great-grandmother was a circuit-riding evangelist. I was born into a long line of leaders. This trait was seen in me even at an early age. I had a homemade nameplate with "Lori Mason" on my bedroom door, just like any business leader would have. Besides leading at school, I led everything I could at church and in my neighborhood. I led my two younger brothers—sometimes as a second, nurturing mom, but mostly as a dictator. My parents said I was "born bossy."

Although the church cultivated my leadership gift and I deeply loved my home church (founded by my father) in New Orleans, I did not see a future for me working in vocational ministry. I watched my mother serve alongside my father and our church by playing the piano, leading the women's ministry and doing a lot of behind-the-scenes work. She sat on the front pew, cheering my dad on through every sermon, and gave me the greatest example of a supportive wife a girl could ever have. I felt I had to either be an itinerate evangelist like some of the women who frequented our church to conduct revivals, or I had to fulfill the role of the typical pastor's wife, which always included playing the piano or the organ (depending on your brand of church). These were the only roles for women in ministry I had modeled for me. Neither role enticed me or lent itself to how I felt I'd been wired. I never saw strategic leadership or entrepreneurship in place in a church setting.

So instead of church ministry, I set out to get a law degree. In my mind, I would practice as an attorney, then rise to become a judge. That is how I envisioned using my bossiness. Little did I know at that time God had very different plans for me that included carrying on the tradition in my family of ministering. And yet here is the great thing: When I stepped into that role, I didn't have to leave my leadership traits behind. On the contrary, God wanted me to use these character traits He had sewn into the fabric of my soul to help accomplish what He wanted. I can still be bossy. I continue to discipline my thoughts and words as a lawyer, and at times must serve as a judge. God did not ask me to surrender these traits just because I am a woman. After all, He is the one who gave me those traits in the first place.

Moving to Austin, Joe said, "This church plant isn't just my vision. It's *our* vision. Whatever God is going to do through us will be because of the prayers that generations of faithful servants of God in your family have prayed." He said, "It's like Joseph and Mary carrying Jesus. Both were needed—Joseph provided the prophetic lineage and Mary physically carried the Savior-baby. God is going to use both of us in our gifts—which are of equal value—to see His vision carried out through us." In that conversation, my strong, manly, and secure husband gave me wings to be the leader God called me to be, and it has set both us and our ministry up to make a huge impact, not only locally but globally with campuses on three continents. Joe is the lead communicator/visionary, and I am the lead strategist/implementor.

WEARING A LEADERSHIP HAT

We've heard the phrase Man Up. In my dad's day, men were expected to work hard at their jobs, be brave, tough, forget about their problems, and "man up," no matter the circumstances. And when they got home, they were to turn their efforts and energies to, as we say in the south, "fixin' things" around the house and other "manly" chores, like lifting heavy boxes, emptying the trash, and opening stuck lids on pickle jars.

So, what does Woman Up really mean? If you look at our society, women tend to fall to one of two extremes. Separated only by one generation, mine has tried to break the mold of our mothers, which commonly deferred to men, even when their position didn't require them to. Even as a strong woman, gifted by God in leadership, and commissioned by my husband, I remember the early days of our ministry when wearing my leadership hat was uncomfortable, especially when it came to leading men who were equally strong and who honestly weren't used to being led by a woman. My "leadership hat" was actually more uncomfortable for them, even though I was the one wearing it. When Joe wasn't with me at the executive team table, I struggled with leading the team through conflict, and they sometimes ran over me. By not stepping into the place of leadership I'd been called to, and by deferring to other leaders just because of their gender, I left a wide-open void for some toxic dynamics and poor leadership decisions to be made that ultimately hurt our organization. I knew mistakes were being made, but I was too insecure to address them.

Young women today have a different struggle—the other extreme. They are rightly not deferring to men just because they're men. But, unfortunately, they fall to the other extreme in the emasculation of men. And young men are, unfortunately, used to being emasculated. If culture shapes beliefs, culture has done a good job of selling men as the weaker, goofier, less responsible, and in many cases, the laughable sex. Women aren't the only ones believing it; so are men. Women seem to be the heroes of this generation, rising up through feminist movements to have equality in their workplaces and homes. While these movements have brought about some very necessary changes, they have also exposed toxic tensions and fueled animosity and unhealthy competition between the sexes. We weren't meant to *compete* with each other but to *complete* each other.

The battle of the sexes started in the first book of the Bible. Eve was created as a solution giver. In Genesis, it refers to her as Adam's "helper," or *ezer* in Hebrew. (We will dive more into the meaning of *ezer* in a later chapter.) You may have heard this before and thought, "Does God really want women to be leaders, including leaders of men? Shouldn't men be the leaders and women be helpers?"

Or you may say, "I don't want to be a leader—that's too much responsibility. I would rather be a behind-the-scenes person than put forth the effort to lead."

Sister, I am the wrong person to share these thoughts with. We have been sold a bill of goods when we think that women's giftings and value are subpar to men's. A woman who does not want to put forth the effort to become the unique person our Lord has made her to be is missing out on fulfilling the calling God has placed on her. The rest of the world needs us to be who God created us to be. I cannot stand by without challenging those who say, "I'm just a woman so I can't ... (fill in the blank)."

Women not only have the ability to lead others—including men—we also have a calling from God to lead in the situations and circumstances He has placed us. If we see ourselves as God has called us to be, we will walk as fierce, unstoppable, confident women. We will square our shoulders, not with arrogance, but as one person put it: *Walking like Elvis and serving like Mother Teresa.*

I want to show you this through one of my great biblical heroes, Judge Deborah.

THE TIME OF JUDGES

There are events in the history of the nation of Israel that anyone who has read the Bible will recall. The births of Isaac, Jacob and the twelve sons of Jacob. Jacob wrestling with an angel who ended the contest by changing Jacob's name to Israel. Israel, all of his children and their families, as well as all of their flocks, moving to Egypt to find food in time of famine. The 400 years the Israelites were slaves to the Egyptians. The calling of Moses through the burning bush and his leading the people of Israel out of Egypt and crossing the Red Sea on dry ground.

Then there are the kings of Israel. Saul, the first king who had his authority stripped when he disobeyed the words of God spoken through the prophet Samuel. David, the giant slayer, who made the nation of Israel great again. Solomon, considered the wisest man of his time, who built a magnificent temple for the Lord.

There is a period of time between the exodus from Egypt and the time of the kings, however, that doesn't get much press. We don't often hear sermons from this period. I'm referring to the time when judges ruled Israel. We find their stories—unsurprisingly—in the Book of Judges in our Bibles. All of the judges from this time were men, except for one. We meet this unique woman in the fourth chapter of Judges.

Deborah was judge at a time when the children of Israel were once again disobeying the good commands of God, worshipping false idols and ignoring the sacrifices God desired. They fell under the control of Jabin, the king of Canaan, and Jabin's military commander, Sisera. Sisera had a large army, including 900 iron chariots (very high tech for that time) that he used to make life miserable for Israel. After twenty years of oppression, the children of Israel cried out to the Lord for help. This is where we meet Deborah.

Deborah held court under a palm tree in the hill country of Ephraim. It was here that the Israelites would come to have her judge their disputes. One day Deborah called for Barak, the leader of Israel's army, to meet her there. Here is a paraphrase of their conversation.

"God has commanded you," said Deborah to Barak, "to take your armies to Mount Tabor and prepare for battle. The Lord will stir up Sisera, who will then bring his army to meet you. And the Lord will win the battle on that day for you and for Israel."

"Okay," said Barak, "I'll do as God has commanded, as long as you go with me."

"I'll go with you," said Deborah. "But know this: The victory will belong to a woman, not to you."

Barak said, "So be it," and off they went. Sisera did arrive with his 900 high tech iron chariots, Barak advanced his armies, and—just as God had said—the Canaanite army was routed. The greatest victory that day did belong to a woman, but not Deborah. (This woman we will meet in a later chapter.) Israel was freed that day from the enemy's oppression and they lived in peace, under the rule of Deborah, for the next forty years.

WOMAN UP IS FOR YOU

GOD DID NOT CREATE YOU TO BE ANYONE'S DOORMAT, AND THAT INCLUDES YOUR OWN. GOD IS CALLING YOU TO WOMAN UP FROM FEAR, SHAME, AND INSECURITY.

"Look," you say, "that's all fine and well for you. You lead at a large, growing church in one of the most popular cities in America. And Deborah, well, she lived thousands of years ago. What does all this have to do with me? I'm just a ... (fill in the blank with your situation)."

What does this have to do with you? Listen up! (This is the "Bossy Me" speaking.) God did not create you to be anyone's doormat, and that includes your own. He has placed leadership qualities in you, and He expects you to use them in the right ways to heal, to guide, to mentor, to set free those who are chafing under the yoke of the Canaanite army with their 900 iron chariots. This is not just a call to a special few women. No matter your past, present, or future, you are called to lead. God is calling you to Woman Up from fear, shame, and insecurity. He invites you to Woman Up from thinking you can't make a difference.

Woman Up and know that:

- God uses women with a past
- God uses women without a past
- God uses women in business
- God uses stay-at-home moms
- God uses those whose kids go to public school
- God uses those who homeschool their children
- God uses single women
- God uses divorced women
- God uses young women
- God uses mature women (notice I did not say old)
- God uses intelligent women

God even uses crazy women. Women who dream huge dreams and see a world where the hurting are healed and the prisoners are set free, if even that world is only within the four walls of her home.

God wants you to Woman Up for His glory. He is calling you, no matter what you or anyone else thinks of you, to be a leader for His sake. This is not a day at the spa. Being the woman in leadership God wants you to be will put you in battles where you will carry scars for the rest of your life. There will be days when you feel like you've gone up against

WHEN YOU FEEL LIKE YOU ARE UP AGAINST 900 CHARIOTS, REMEMBER THAT OBEDIENCE ALWAYS WINS.

900 iron chariots. You will fall and have to learn to get back up. But the rewards—oh, the rewards! You will see the favor that comes with obedience. You will see the profit that comes from using your gifts, instead of making excuses for them. You will be comfortable in your

own skin, free to be who you are without fear that you are too much or not enough. You will see a legacy birthed in your family that will produce generational blessings. You will see your influence grow. Leaders will seek your counsel. Friends and neighbors will come to you to ask how they can have the contentment and radiance they see in you, even in the most difficult of times. Most of all, you will come to know God. You will know Him not as we imagine Him to be, but as He truly is.

And what can be more rewarding than that?

So put your big girl panties on and let's Woman Up!

CHAPTER 2

GET UP

Then Deborah said to Barak, "Up!"

Judges 4:14 (NRSV)

"A sunset shows that life is too beautiful to hold on to the past,
so move on to the present."

—Unknown

Life as I knew it suddenly ended on March 27, 1988.

It was a beautiful Palm Sunday morning in New Orleans. I was worshipping, along with my two younger brothers, in the small church my parents had founded many years before, and where I heard my dad preach most every Sunday. Bill Mason was a giant of a man in my eyes. He was a great preacher who knew his Bible inside and out. He wasn't concerned with building a bigger church—he cared about building up those who were entrusted to his care.

Many times, we made room at our table for the less fortunate, and people were abundantly blessed by my mom's wonderful Cajun cooking. Sometimes we even gave up our beds so people could temporarily live with us while they got back on their feet. Home visits, hospital visits, and giving people rides to and from church were just what we did as a family. As my parents would say, "This is what being the Body of Christ is all about." Under our father's guidance and led by his example, we learned what compassion and caring looked like. And every day, Dad reminded us that God had handpicked us to lead His sheep, to love His people. He told us over and over that there is no greater privilege or calling than to shepherd the sheep God brought our way.

My father was dedicated to his church, but all the more to his family. He modeled true love in how he treated Mom—always with respect, always with loving admiration. And he loved us kids with a fatherly love that echoed the love of our Heavenly Father. I remember one Sunday when I was in high school. I had always been a very expressive, passionate worshipper, clapping, lifting my hands, and singing loudly to praise our God. This particular Sunday I decided I wanted to "fit in" better with the teens around me. So, when the music began, I sang, but in a quieter voice. I clapped, but without enthusiasm. My hands stayed at my side instead of being lifted up toward our Father. *No big deal,* I thought. *After all, I'm still here in church, right?*

That night I woke in the early hours of the morning feeling very thirsty. I went to the kitchen to get a glass of water, and while there I heard someone in the next room. It was Dad, and he was praying. Praying for *me*.

"Oh God," he cried, "don't let my daughter lose her passion for You. Don't let her stop pursuing You, stop praising You with her whole heart." I could picture him pacing the floor in the next room or maybe even on his face, crying as he sought God on my behalf. *What's the big deal?* I thought. *All I did was not clap like I usually do.* But Dad could see in my heart, the tiny spark of self-determination and self-consciousness that, left to itself, would grow into a fire whose smoke would smother my passion for Jesus. Believe me, the next Sunday I was back to my "usual" self, taking the lead in worship among my friends. I knew the concern Dad had for my soul—I could hear it and feel it in his prayer for me.

Back to March of 1988. I was home from college on that fateful Sunday—it was the beginning of Spring Break. Our station wagon was fully packed to spend a few days together at a Texas pastors' conference, where us kids would get to hang out at the pool while our parents spent the day in church services. That's called a "vacation" in a pastor's family, and we were super excited to all be together at a nice hotel. Before we were to leave, we were together in the church founded by my parents, worshiping together as we always did. That Palm Sunday we sang with gratitude for how Jesus showed Himself as the Way, the Truth, and the Life on His way to the Cross. We sang with expectation for what Jesus would do the next Sunday—His glorious resurrection. After we sang, and then greeted one another, we composed ourselves to hear a message from Dad about Jesus. Always about Jesus.

Then ... halfway through his message, Dad suddenly stopped speaking. He froze for just an instant, and then collapsed. He suffered a massive heart attack. I was unprepared for the shock and then for the emptiness I felt as my father was lifted into the back of an ambulance to be taken to the hospital, where we were given the news a short while later that he was "dead on arrival" and that they'd tried with no success to revive him. How could my life go on? Who would be there to walk me down the aisle when I got married? Who would be "Papa Bill" to my children? It then came to me: Who would lead this church he worked so hard to build? In fact, I remember telling my aunt on the way home from the hospital, "We aren't in ministry any more ... and we never will be again." I had no idea, until that moment, how much being involved in my parents' ministry had shaped my identity. I wasn't just a pastor's daughter. I was a part of a family who led our church. Without my father, who would shepherd the people who made up the church, who depended on my parents to help them through the "everydayness" of life? The church that had always meant so much to our lives now was the place of pain and death.

Mom did what she could to keep us going. We worshipped around the piano in three-part harmony in our living room to strengthen ourselves so that we could continue ministering to others as a family, even though we were reeling in our own pain and loss. Yet, for me, the emptiness was just too much. There was a season of probably six months where I would refer to myself as a "walking dead person," numb and unable to fully express emotions. As a leader and first-born child, I put upon myself the burden of making sure my mom and brothers were healing while I tucked away my own grief to be faced at a later date. I continued to show up every time the church doors opened, even though I felt I was just going through the motions, and that the songs I sang were just hitting the ceiling. God saw the depths of my heart, overlooking the numbness that enveloped me, and began to fan that spark of love for Him and His people that was buried deep within me. Over time, the church became the greatest place of healing for me and for all of us ... the place where all three of us kids eventually realized that we, too, were called to follow the example of our parents set for us, to love and shepherd God's people. What seemed like the end was just the beginning.

REAL STRENGTH IS CONTINUING TO GET UP, EVEN WHEN NOTHING IN YOU FEELS LIKE GOING ON.

There are defining moments in all of our lives, days that will make you want to give up. The difference in outcome is continuing to get up, even when nothing in you feels like going on. When I said, "I guess we'll never be in ministry again," I was tying my future to my father, who had just passed away. How many times do we feel like our future is shattered because someone or something died, or because someone walked out of our lives, or because we feel like we made the ultimate mistake? I had to make a decision, one that would hold my future. I knew that whatever decision I made would set the course for the rest of my life. This was not something I did carelessly. But I knew I needed to make up my mind what my life was going to look like from here on out. So, I did. I made up my mind.

I decided not to give up but to get up and go on.

Fast forward thirty years. I now lead, alongside my husband, a dynamic house of worship, healing, and life in Texas, while my two wonderful brothers each pastor churches of their own. What motivates us to provide a place of belonging in our churches is that we found healing and belonging in our home church, even when life was the darkest. Out of death, now there is life. Out of that small but mighty church, we three Mason kids are all pastoring churches where thousands come to hear about The Hope—Jesus—to any hopeless situation.

TO LEARN THE ART OF WAR

Somehow, erroneous and dangerous teaching has wormed its way into churches today; teaching that says those who follow the Lord will walk on smooth, straight roads, lined with beautiful and unfading flowers on either side. This teaching leads people to believe life is to be all king cake and sweet tea. This is not at all what Jesus and the apostles taught. Jesus told his followers that *"in this world you will have trouble"* (John 16:33 NIV). He also told His followers He did not come *"to bring peace, but a sword"* (Matthew 10:34). In 2 Corinthians, Paul writes about some of the hardships he faced while preaching the gospel, including being whipped, stoned, shipwrecked, and starved. Far from protecting us from any and all hardship, God often allows us to experience difficulties in order to strengthen us and prepare us for the roles He has planned for us. He wants us to learn the art of warfare, fighting against our own fears, wrong desires, and laziness to pursue holiness, being made into the likeness of Jesus. There is biblical precedence for this found in the Old Testament. We see that the Lord put enemies in the path of the Israelites as they entered Canaan—the Promised Land—so they could learn the art of warfare. We read in Judges, chapter three, verses 1 and 2 (I am quoting here from *The Message*):

These are the nations that GOD left there, using them to test the Israelites who had no experience in the Canaanite wars. He did it to train the descendants of Israel, the ones who had no battle experience, in the art of war.

God purposely left enemy nations in the land of Canaan so that the Israelites would have to fight. Remember, before the Jews crossed over into the Promised Land, they had only known the life of nomads in the wilderness of Egypt. There were no enemies to fight, no land to conquer in the wilderness. Now God expected them to go forth and destroy the enemy nations in order for the Israelites to live where God had called them to live. First, they were going to have to learn how to be soldiers and leaders. God needed mighty warriors to carry out His will, and so He left nations in the land the Israelites would have to drive out with war.

Whenever I've felt like I'm in a battle, I remind myself of Psalm 144:1, *"Blessed be the Lord, my rock, who trains my hands for war, and my fingers for battle."* You've heard of "on-the-job training"? My experience is that we have "in-the-battle training." But thank God, our Warrior-King is right by our side.

This brings us to Deborah the judge who held court under a palm tree in Ephraim. Deborah was not just wise—a quality all good judges must possess—she was a prophetess, one who proclaimed the message God gave her to share. And before she could share what God said, she had to hear God clearly, right? Deborah had to have a relationship with the Lord where she learned to hear His voice above all other voices.

We first meet Deborah sitting under her palm tree having just heard from the Lord. God told her to call Barak and tell him he was to raise an army and get them in position to fight the Canaanites. Spoiler alert: Israel defeats the Canaanites! But before this happens, Barak is faced with his own insecurities and fears.

"I'll go and do as the Lord commands," said Barak to Deborah, "but only if you go with me. If you won't go, then I won't go." Barak knew the wisdom and strength Deborah had and which he lacked. He submitted himself to the woman God placed in leadership for such as time as this.

"Oh," replied Deborah, "I'll go with you, but know this. A woman will receive the glory for the battle, not you."

Let's take a time out. If we read this in today's context, we can interpret it as Deborah getting snarky with Barak, playing the gender card and positioning herself as superior. We can read into it an attitude that is inconsistent with the story as a whole. I submit that Deborah, a woman of wisdom and understanding, a woman who had the "sons of Israel" lining up to hear her judgments, was actually being sensitive to his manhood. She was encouraging him to count the cost, to recognize that he could be criticized for needing a woman to "hold his hand" in battle. In her concern for him, she actually secured even more of his trust. She didn't have any ambition to position herself as a hero in battle. She had his best interest in mind. I call it a "circle of security" Because she was secure, Barak did not feel threatened by her strength. Because he didn't feel threatened by her strength, he invited her to lead alongside him.

There are at least two other instances where we see this circle of security.

One is the Proverbs 31 woman, whom we will meet later. The other is the story of Esther. A king who'd been publicly rejected and shamed before all of his leaders by Queen Vashti (who was then banished and replaced by Esther), a king who'd been manipulated by his second in command, a king who had every right to have trust issues, is healed by the courageous act and wisdom of God given through Esther. He is so restored in his security and is able to trust Esther so much that he says to Esther, "What is your wish, Queen Esther? It shall be granted you. And what is your request? *Even to the half of my kingdom, it shall be fulfilled.*" Her selflessness saved her people from death and freed her husband from the toxic relationship with a brutal leader who had positioned himself to take advantage of the king.

GREAT LEADERS INSPIRE COURAGE AND GREATNESS IN OTHERS.

You don't become a great leader because of a title or a position. You become a great leader by inspiring courage and greatness in others. In fact, Deborah was called a prophetess. Depending on our spiritual backgrounds, we can have differing views of how that looks. (It is sometimes wacky or spooky.) The primary characteristic of the prophetic is not to predict what someone will eat for breakfast tomorrow or even to expose someone's faults; it is a gift of inspiration that confirms the direction of God for someone's life, and it will always line up with God's Word. I believe that, as women, God has gifted us to be more sensitive to the voice of God. We need to steward the gift to cheer people on as they pursue God's purpose.

Now back to Deborah and Barak: Off they went, gathering an army to them as they traveled to where God said they were to assemble. We read in Judges chapter four that ten thousand warriors *went up* behind Barak, and that Deborah *went up* with him. Where did they go? They went *up*! God is waiting for us to *get up* and *go up* before He uses us to defeat our enemies.

When the commander of the Canaanite army, Sisera, heard the Israelites raised an army, he brought out a much larger army—along with those 900 iron chariots—and dared Barak to attack. We

LOOK BEYOND PEOPLE'S POSITION AND SEE THEIR POTENTIAL.

don't know precisely where Barak was at this time, but one thing we know is that he was down. Perhaps he was in his tent, in the fetal position, with a pillow over his head. Maybe he was hiding in a cave. Maybe he was on his knees praying for God's direction which God had already clearly given. Wherever Barak was, he was *down*—he wasn't in battle position. When Deborah found him, she had one word for Barak: "Up!" She saw Barak's posture was one of fear. The first thing out of her mouth was, "Get up! For this is the day God is going to give Sisera and his army into your hand. And the Lord is indeed going before you in this battle." Deborah looked beyond his *position* and saw his *potential*. But Barak could not begin to fulfill that potential while he was down—he first had to get up.

Joe and I recently had dinner with a couple in our church, and we were so moved by their unexpected love story. They met online—that's not the unexpected part. This very successful, confident, and attractive couple began to tell us how her first marriage had tragically broken her. She came to the U.S. as a collegiate athlete. At 6'4", built like a specimen of athleticism, it's not surprising that she also played basketball on two European Olympic teams. Unfortunately, while in college, she met and married a man addicted to substances who would physically and emotionally abuse her for years. Finally, he died of complications of his addiction, but not before leaving her a shell of a woman. This brilliant and beautiful woman—who speaks four different languages—apprehensively decided to try again at love and met her second husband. Her second husband described her to me as someone who was very insecure when he met her. When they first became acquainted, she was working in a field surrounded by men who were often uncomfortable with her success and her physical stature. After several months of long-distance communication, he traveled to meet her in person, and what did he bring her? A pair of beautiful high-heeled shoes! He wasn't intimidated by her strength or stature, even though she is much taller than he is.

Some "Deborah's" aren't women. They are people—men and women—who cause you to stop shrinking (physically or emotionally) and to stand tall. They celebrate your uniqueness.

I've had the opportunity to be with some incredible leaders who impact countless people in the ministry and corporate world. Their resumes could intimidate most anyone. Yet, the best of them never leave you the way they found you. They inspire confidence, they make you feel like you are bigger than you are and that you can do more than you think you can!

MY DEBORAH

Joe and I were the new pastors of a well-established church in a very small town in Louisiana. There were 300 members at this church, which may not sound like much until you consider there were only 500 people living in the town, and only around 8,000 in the surrounding communities. But coming from an even smaller church, it was intimidating for a girl in her mid-twenties. Add to that Eileen, the previous pastor's wife. It seemed that every time I would talk with a woman in the church, she would find a way to say, "Oh, we miss Eileen." Over and over I heard how much this woman was missed with the implication that I was no Eileen. They loved Joe as their pastor. I would often hear someone saying, "We just love Pastor Joe, but"—wait for it—"we really miss Eileen."

Believe me, that got old very fast. One day I remember distinctly thinking, "I'd like to be Eileen too, but I'm twenty-four, not fifty, and I'm still trying to work out being an adult, let alone being the mother figure of a church whose members are twice my age." I went to see my good friend Mica, a woman who was about fifteen years older than me whom I had grown to love and respect in a very short time. She was a leader in our church, a tremendous teacher of God's Word, who could quote the Bible backward and forward. She was also a brilliant business woman, a veterinarian, a great wife, and a mother of teenagers. I could depend on her for honest, godly feedback. She was remodeling her house at the time and didn't have any furniture, so we were sitting on the floor. I looked at Mica and blurted out, "I knew I couldn't be a pastor's wife. I knew I didn't have the right personality. These people hate me." In my heart I knew they didn't hate me. They loved me, but had a strange way of saying it, and they definitely loved Eileen more. I was waiting for Mica to say, "No, you are never going to be like Eileen." I wanted my friend to confirm my negative feelings about myself to make me feel better about being so down.

But instead Mica said, "God has not called Eileen to be here now. He picked you. He called Eileen and her husband to go to another city. You are the woman He has called. Are you going to step up into God's calling or not?"

That day changed my life. A Deborah spoke into my life. Mica didn't say, "You have every reason to be sad," any more than Deborah told Barak, "You have every reason to be afraid. Stay down." Mica didn't say that to me. She said, in essence, "Get up!" We all need people who are willing to boldly speak words of encouragement and direction to us. It may not be what we want to hear, but if this person has the spirit of Deborah, they will be the words we need to hear if we are to carry out God's design for us. If we don't have Deborah's speaking to us, we will never get up off the floor, out of bed, out of our cave. We will only hear the enemy saying to us, "You weren't really called. God can't use you. You aren't good enough, strong enough, godly enough. Just stay down where no one will see how pitiful you really are."

We sometimes fear that response because we've experienced that response. Many of us have felt the pain from people who kicked us while we were down, or stepped on us on the way to the top. When the twelve spies went into the Promised Land (see Numbers 13), ten of them, all but Joshua and Caleb, felt small.

Numbers 13:31-33: *"We are not able to go up against the people, for they are stronger than we are." So they brought to the people of Israel a bad report of the land that they had spied out, saying, "The land, through which we have gone to spy it out, is a land that devours its inhabitants, and all the people that we saw in it are of great height. And there we saw the Nephilim (the sons of Anak, who come from the Nephilim), and we seemed to ourselves like grasshoppers, and so we seemed to them."*

SOMETIMES YOUR PROBLEMS WILL SEEM BIGGER THAN GOD'S PROMISE.

They felt like the size of grasshoppers, to be exact, dwarfed by who they faced. Perhaps they'd never overcome the mentality of slavery from all of the years their people had experienced in captivity to Egypt. Their problems seemed bigger than their promise. The giants seemed bigger than the God who had supernaturally delivered them from captivity to Egypt; the God who parted the Red Sea and drowned their pursuers; the God who provided water from a rock and manna from Heaven to feed them; and the God who led them by a cloud and by fire to the very place where they now questioned their ability to enter in. Thank God for a leader like Caleb who reminded them—who stood in agreement with God—and said,

"...Let us go up at once and occupy it, for we are well able to overcome it" (verse 30).

Caleb had a "Get Up" spirit that Barak lacked.

We really don't know much about Barak before he was called by God to lead an army into war. But we do know he was down and Deborah commanded him to get up, and on that day Barak's army routed Sisera's army. We only read of Barak one more time in Scripture—in what is called the "Faith Hall of Fame," Hebrews chapter eleven. There we read that Barak—though faith—conquered kingdoms, won strength out of weakness, and became mighty in war. And it was all because Deborah was the leader she was called to be and boldly told Barak, "Get up!"

CHAPTER 3

BACK UP

He has removed our sins as far from us
as the east is from the west.

Psalm 103:12 (NLT)

"There is no saint without a past,
and no sinner without a future."

—Saint Augustine of Hippo

I've always loved hearing about and seeing firsthand people transformed from sinners to saints. My parents had a coffee shop ministry on Bourbon Street, where I got to witness many trophies of God's grace, hearing testimonies of things I sometimes didn't understand until I got older. We would spend Mardi Gras singing praise songs from a balcony overlooking the madness and passing out tracts and sharing the love of Jesus on the streets to those who were open to receiving. I never have had a testimony like the ones I heard back then, which is the greatest testimony of all—not one of perfection by any means but one I attribute to the wonderful, godly home I grew up in, our commitment to church, and the keeping power of God.

I watched as ex-convicts, drug addicts, prostitutes, and some of the French Quarter's most infamous female impersonators received freedom. I knew it was possible to be forgiven from even the greatest of sins, yet I still experienced the power shame can have over a person. I remember the first time I experienced it; it was over the silliest situation. In first grade, I had long hair, a new pair of scissors, and a little "friend" named RJ who dared me to cut a piece of my hair—a piece so small that it was completely unnoticeable. He then told my teacher (who looked for every opportunity to be mean!), and I was reprimanded in front of the whole class. Feeling a sense of power, RJ threatened to tell my mom, and made me believe that it would be an even bigger deal to my parents. My imagination went wild with what kind of repercussions this could cause in my family— would my parents ever forgive me? Could they love me after this level of disobedience? I realized quickly I could be blackmailed and so did RJ. Each day I'd bring him pocket change I'd found lying around or a toy from my two-year-old brother's small collection—a Matchbox car, an action figure, or a Happy Meal prize. The guilt compounded because I was not only a rebellious haircutter, but now I was robbing my precious little brother and living a life of deception to my parents. Each night I'd ask God's forgiveness, but when I looked in the mirror, I saw a "bad girl." I kept giving myself deadlines to come clean with my parents. "By next month, by Christmas, before my next birthday..." I had become a slave to my fear of what would happen if I was "found out."

Months, maybe a year or more went by, even after RJ and I were in different classes and a new year of school had begun. One day, the right opportunity came. My parents had out-of-town company sitting around the kitchen table and my grandmother had come to pick me up to spend a day at her house. As I was leaving the house, and kissing my mom good-bye, I whispered in her ear, "In first grade, I cut my hair!" My mom laughed, "It's okay, baby. Have a fun day!" What? That's it? No punishment? No reprimand? None, never another word about it. Just like that, I was free.

I wonder how many people are walking around enslaved to their past—whether it's cutting their hair without permission or committing a sin that seems unforgivable. Despite the many examples in the Bible of Jesus saving demoniacs, prostitutes, thieves, murderers, adulterers, and a woman who'd had five husbands and was shacking up with number six, sometimes we can be talked into thinking that we are the only ones not eligible for His saving grace. We think our sin is bigger than God's forgiveness. I have some good news. You can't out-sin God's salvation. If you whisper your sin into the ear of God, He won't turn you away. He'll say, "It's okay, baby! You're covered." He will never bring it up again. Just like that, you will be free.

Here's some more good news. God doesn't just want to redeem you. He wants to redeem your story. God actually rewrites stories. He always has, always will. Let's look at a couple of life stories that underwent God's editing.

GUS AND ANGIE

Gus was a partier, no doubt about it. Drinking, women, and more drinking was the routine for Gus, even to the age of thirty. Life for him was a ceaseless party. He fathered a child with his live-in girlfriend, and then refused to marry her when he thought he had the opportunity to marry a different woman who had just inherited a very large amount of money. Eating and drinking—especially drinking—was his "occupation." When the beer ran out, he went in search of the next gathering with more of the "liquid gold" he consumed constantly. His father, who was not a Christian, paid little attention to Gus's lifestyle. "He is what he is" was his father's only comment. But Gus's mother, Monica, was a devout Christian who prayed continually for Gus to repent of his ways, give up his partying life, and become a follower of Jesus.

Never, ever underestimate the power of a praying mama.

Gus did convert at the age of thirty-one. He had always been a deep thinker, even when he was drunk. Now that he was sober, he put his mind to work to understand who Jesus is and how to apply what Scripture teaches to everyday life. He became a renowned Christian leader, teacher, and evangelist. He wrote many books of his experiences and insights into the Bible. And his teachings shaped a still young church to withstand the onslaughts of the world. Gus—better known as St. Augustine—was a man with a past as dark as night. But darkness doesn't stand a chance when Jesus—who is the Light—comes into one's life.

Angie was born into a Christian family and raised in the faith. Yet soon after reaching adulthood, she began her quest for material wealth and fame. She married a man of high social standing and gave birth over time to several children, yet neglected her family for the continued pursuit of riches. She was a shopaholic; she couldn't pass a store without wanting to buy something to make her seem to be a woman of status. Then a godly counselor came into Angie's life and, by sharing Scripture and wisdom with her, led her to repent of her greed and focus on Jesus.

Did everything go great for Angie from that point? No. Shortly after recommitting her life to Jesus, her husband and all of her children died. Though grieving, Angie kept her eyes on the Lord. She became a nurse and served the poor and hurting, often begging for food for their needs. Angie—better known as Angela of Foligno (Italy)—died in 1309, but left behind a legacy of leading the poor to health, wellness, and—most important of all—faith in Jesus.

We all have things in our past we wish we could forget. Some pasts are much more complicated than others, like those of Augustine and Angela of Foligno. Others have a past known only to a few people, but a damaged past nonetheless. We all have done things—or maybe haven't done things—we regret. But this cannot keep you from being the godly leader you are called to be—unless you yourself cling to your past instead of walking in the present with hope for the future. Rick Warren, author of *The Purpose Driven Life*, says, "We are products of our past, but we don't have to be prisoners of it."

There are those who cling to their broken past as a badge of honor. You know the kind. They want to constantly talk about things they did or things done to them decades ago. Their past has become the only life they know. If they were to let go of the hurts done to them long ago, they would feel like a ghost of themselves. Have you ever noticed that there are people who are doing incredible things for God who had the darkest past, while there are others who can't get past much smaller hurdles or offenses? They've become comfortable in their own dysfunction and continue to repeat patterns of behavior that keep them from a victorious life. Yet there is hope. Through Christ, you can go from being a victim to a victor. Is it easy? No. But you *can* do it. Hebrews 12:1 encourages us to *"lay aside every weight, and sin which clings so closely, and let us run with endurance the race that is set before us."* The weight many need to lay aside is their past.

WE'VE GOT TO GIVE UP TO GO UP.

We've got to give up to go up.

There's a crippling teaching that gives excessive freedom to sin, ignoring the many scriptural teachings that provoke us to leave behind the past. It replaces "obedience" with the wrong definition of grace. Grace doesn't license us; it empowers us to live up to God's purpose and calling. We aren't saved by works, yet when Christ takes up residence in our hearts, we can't help but realize there's a change in our desires, our thoughts, our behaviors, and our motives.

Titus 2:12 (NIV) says the grace of God *"teaches us to say 'No' to ungodliness and worldly passions, and to live self-controlled, upright and godly lives in this present age."*

When Jesus encountered the woman caught in adultery, He rescued her from those who would shame and stone her. Then in John 8:10-11, *Jesus stood up and said to her, "Woman, where are they? Has no one condemned you?" She said, "No one, Lord." And Jesus said, "Neither do I condemn you; go, and from now on sin no more."*

Notice Jesus didn't say, "Keep up the adultery!" He stepped in, He showed mercy when she did nothing to earn it, and then He said, *"From now on sin no more."* I'm thankful for the order of that exchange. He didn't ask her if she planned to continue to sin before He granted mercy. He unconditionally granted it, but He is too loving to leave us where He found us. He empowers us to progress.

Across our church campuses, people wear shirts and carry signs in the parking lot that say, "You Belong Here." We want everyone, no matter their back story or their present condition, to know they are welcomed in our doors. We realize that sometimes people think they'll be struck by lightning when they enter a church building. But, we say, "You won't be struck by lightning, you'll be struck by the grace of God!" You shouldn't just stop at belonging. Your *belonging* should turn into your *becoming*. First time guests wouldn't quite understand it if they read it on a t-shirt, but what should be on our shirts is "You *Become* Here!" Through the Word of God and through relationships in the Body of Christ, we are all in a constant state of becoming, and we will never arrive.

PROVOKING GOD

How would it be if your dad was king of a very large land, a land with all kinds of good things to eat and drink (including grapes so big it took two strong men just to carry a bunch), mountains and caves to explore, and a sea to swim in? And then your father, the king, said all you had to do was to stick with what he told you to do, for everything he instructed you to do was for your ultimate good. Then you could freely enjoy the treasures of his land. But instead of doing what your kind and loving father asked you to do, you rebelled against him and started imitating people in the neighboring cities, people who hated your dad and who were his enemies. Not a very wise path to walk, right?

This is what the children of Israel did once they reached the Promised Land. We read about their disobedience in Judges.

> *And the people of Israel did what was evil in the sight of the LORD and served the Baals. And they abandoned the LORD, the God of their fathers, who had brought them out of the land of Egypt. They went after other gods, from among the gods of the peoples who were around them, and bowed down to them. And they provoked the LORD to anger* (Judges 2:11-12).

If there's one person in the entire universe you don't want mad at you, it's God. One of the characteristics of God is that He is slow to get angry and overflowing with love toward each of us (see Psalm 103:8). You have to work hard to get Him to be angry with you, and it seems the Israelites were working overtime to do just that. Talk about a past.

God allowed their enemies, the ones the Jews thought were so cool, to move in and steal what had been given them by the Lord. These enemies persecuted and oppressed the Jews so fiercely that the Jews would cry out to the Lord for help and promise to obey Him if only He would deliver them. So, God raised up judges to deliver the Israelites out of the hands of their enemies. For a while, things would be fine. But when the judge would die, we read that the Jews *"would relapse and behave worse than their ancestors, following other gods, worshipping them and bowing down to them ... "* (Judges 2:19 NRSV).

Each time the Israelites turned away, God would stir up their enemies and Israel would be oppressed once again. Then God would hear their cries, raise up a judge to rescue them, and when that judge would die, the Israelites would fall back into their pattern of sin.

Can you relate to this? Do you find yourself falling into a pattern of sin that makes you its prisoner? And you call out to the Lord who forgives and delivers you, making you free once again, only to slip right back into this pattern of sin. An endless string of judges could not help the Jews break the power of sin—just as listening to endless sermons cannot deliver us from a cycle of sin in our lives. Paul, in the book of Romans, expresses his frustration with falling back into sin even though he desired to live a holy life.

"I've tried everything and nothing works. I'm at the end of my rope. Is there no one who can do anything for me?" Isn't that the real question?

And after posing this question, Paul goes on.

"The answer, thank God, is that Jesus Christ can and does." Paul says Jesus, through the Holy Spirit, ends the conflict between our desire to walk faithfully with the Lord and the influence sin has over our lives. We are now freed from the pull of sin, free to walk with Jesus in our lives.

In Proverbs 24:16 it says, *"For the righteous falls seven times and rises again...."* No matter your struggle today, find the courage to get up again. When you've disappointed others and yourself, take heart. There is forgiveness. God can and will restore you ... once more. When all you have left is Him, you have everything you need to start over again.

NEVER COMPROMISE GOD'S CALL FOR YOUR COMFORT.

As Churchill said, "Success is never final, nor is failure ever fatal. It is the courage to continue that counts in the end."

When we built our current Celebration Church building, we built it in a very traditional town with very traditional ideas, a town that didn't reflect the culture of the rest of Austin. There were those who came to visit us and saw me in a leadership position. Some of those who only knew a traditional way of "doing church" left and never came back. This was disheartening to say the least. Yet I knew God called me to lead. I couldn't compromise God's calling for my comfort. I had to stay the course.

Don't let your failures define who you are. This is not God's plan for any of us. Jesus lived a sinless, holy life, blazing a trail for us to follow in our pursuit of a holy life that brings glory to God. His death on the Cross broke the power sin had over each one of us. This should make us want to pause right now and take a praise break! He rescued us. He freed us, so that we no longer have to live in bondage to our past. It's good for us to check our hearts that we don't lose the awe of what He did for us.

A LEADER IS PROVEN IN DOWN TIMES

The cycle of disobedience to God, destruction by enemy nations, and delivery through the judges God gave to Israel became the hallmark of the Jews. This is when we meet Deborah the judge. We don't know much about her past. We read she was married to a man named Lappidoth (seriously? What did she call him at home—Lappy?), but we don't read about any children. Perhaps Deborah carried the shame of being barren as her past. Today, we understand that the inability to conceive is a medical problem that can often be overcome with medication, special fertility treatments, and counseling. In biblical times, however, barrenness was considered punishment from God. If you were a woman without children, you were looked at as shameful, a heavy burden to carry indeed. If Deborah was barren (and we don't know either way), she did not let the social shame keep her from becoming the leader God intended for her to be.

Let's look again at Deborah's leadership in rescuing Israel from their oppressor, starting with the reason the Jews were being oppressed to begin with.

And the people of Israel again did what was evil in the sight of the LORD after Ehud died. And the LORD sold them into the hand of Jabin king of Canaan, who reigned in Hazor. The commander of his army was Sisera, who lived in Harosheth-ha-goyim. Then the people of Israel cried out to the LORD for help, for he had 900 chariots of iron and he oppressed the people of Israel cruelly for twenty years (Judges 4:1-3).

IT'S NOT *FAKING* IT, IT'S *FAITHING* IT! LEADERS GIVE UP THE RIGHT TO COMPLETELY FALL APART EVERY TIME THEY FEEL LIKE IT.

Deborah was a judge in a very down time for her country. It's much easier to lead in an "up" time—you can almost do that on cruise control. It's much harder when those you are called to lead are down. Down times prove a leader. Have you ever had to put on a happy face when things are falling apart? I've led worship and ministered my heart out when on the inside I felt surrounded by enemies; when I felt like things were falling apart, during very difficult times. On one occasion a member of our team was trying to cause a church split by sabotaging things behind the scenes. He was calling people in our church and spreading negativity about how we made decisions. One Sunday, I looked out in the audience and saw people with arms crossed, staring at me with a hateful countenance. I never let them see how hurt I was, because there were other people in the room who needed to be encouraged by that service, not distracted by a discouraged leader.

It's not *faking* it, it's *faithing* it—this is what I told myself that morning. As a leader, you give up the right to completely fall apart every time you feel like it.

As a mom, there have been times when I didn't know how we'd pay our bills, yet my kids never had a clue that we were struggling—they aren't equipped to handle that kind of pressure. When you are responsible for others, sometimes you just have to power through the difficulties and lead yourself and others to the winning side.

GO UP, AND CALL OTHERS TO COME UP WITH YOU.

Deborah had to first get up herself, and then lead others to get up. Deborah's "court" was held under a palm tree on a hill, and the Israelites had to go *up* to present their case or seek her wisdom. She did not dwell *down* in a valley where she couldn't be seen. She was up where she could be seen by all. If she had any shame or hurts in her past, they did not prevent her from daily going up and calling others to come up with her.

Deborah called Barak to come up to her. There she told him the Lord said for Barak to raise an army of 10,000 warriors to go to war with Jabin and his commander, Sisera. Deborah told Barak the Lord would deliver Sisera into his hands. When Barak asked Deborah to come with him, she said she would, but the Lord was going to then deliver Sisera into the hands of a woman. Just who was this woman whom God was going to use to defeat this strong enemy? Hint: It was a woman with a past that could have kept her from being the deliverer the Israelites needed.

God no longer looks at your past, and you shouldn't either. He removes your sins as far as the east is from the west, which is another way of saying "to infinity and beyond"! It is time for us to back up and see that God has always had us in His hand and His heart. There is no excuse for not being the woman God intends for you to be. My sister, Back Up—then Woman Up so you can Get Up!

CHAPTER 4

COURAGE UP

Do not be afraid or discouraged, for the LORD will
personally go ahead of you. He will be with you;
he will neither fail you nor abandon you.

Deuteronomy 31:8 (NLT)

"I'm learning that the true meaning of 'woman up' means
to continue to put one foot in front of the other,
moving forward, ever moving forward regardless of fear
or the unknown. Moving forward, sometimes half a day
at a time, sometimes one moment at a time."

—Maureen O'Brien

I had three primary fears as I was growing up. The first came, in part, from my Pentecostal heritage. I was very afraid of missing the rapture. We were taught to believe if we committed a sin—or even thought about sinning—at the moment Jesus came back, He would leave us behind. When the *Left Behind* book series came out, my friends all said, "You just have to read these." I replied, "No, I *don't* have to read those books. I've lived them all my life!"

My senior year of high school my parents surprised me by allowing me to go to the prom at my school. "As long as you go with a Christian boy," my mom said. There was a nice Christian boy I liked, and he liked me, so with my parents' blessings we made plans to go to the dance together. Then, a few days before the big day I got a phone call from my grandmother. Nanny was a Pentecostal Holiness preacher in a small church—called the Prayer Mission Church—in the very small town of Tecumseh, Oklahoma. Nanny rarely called to talk with me, and when she did, I would be scared. She had fire in her voice that made me shake. This time, however, she sounded as if she were about to cry.

"Uh, hi Nanny," I said, shivering. "How are you?"

"Oh Lori," she said, "I'm not good. I've been praying for you all week. I'm fasting and praying for you."

"Okay, thank you," I said, "but why are you doing this for me?" I didn't think my dad had told her about my plans for prom. I was wrong.

"I heard you are going to that dance on Friday night. I'm praying Jesus doesn't come back right then because He is not going to rapture you off the dance floor."

So, in addition to the beautiful dress my parents bought me, I wore a bit of fear to the prom. I would dance a little, because I love to dance. Then I would remember my grandmother's words and would sneak off by myself and pray, "Jesus, please, please come into my heart," just in case she was right. When the night was over, I rejoiced that I had made it through. Jesus had not returned, and I had not been left behind on the dance floor.

My second fear growing up was just as irrational as the first. I had a great fear of being kidnapped. My other grandmother lived in constant fear of one of her kids or grandkids being kidnapped. She reminded me every time I went outside to play that any car passing by was probably driven by a kidnapper. Each time a car drove by, I contorted my face into as ugly a shape as I could just so the kidnappers would think, "Surely there's a cuter kid I could pick up."

Seriously, that's what I did.

I think my mom finally found out what was happening (because she had experienced the same things as a child), and convinced her mother to stop terrorizing me with those thoughts, so that I could enjoy a normal childhood, playing in my front yard.

The third fear that haunted me through my childhood was showing up to school without my clothes on. Have you ever had that dream where you are sitting in class and all of a sudden realize you are naked? That fear has stuck with me to this day. A few weeks before beginning to write this, I dreamed I was speaking at a women's conference with no pants on. Most people shrug off these dreams as just too much pizza the night before, but in my mind, it was very real. Wherever I went, I kept checking to see if I was still wearing clothes.

That dream, of course, comes when we fear we are not properly prepared for an event about to happen. To compensate for this fear, I overprepare and overthink. One day my son Connor "subtly" sent me a TED talk he had recently watched. When I didn't immediately watch the link he'd sent, he decided to do his own intervention. He said, "Mom, you're not a procrastinator—you're a *pre*crastinator. This talk is all about people who overthink, overprepare; people who arrive no later than fifteen minutes early. Mom, this is you!"

Our fears and our past experiences often drive our behavior, causing us to overcompensate for past failures. Throughout my life, I've had wonderful people who were (let me put it gently and not name names) less than punctual. In elementary school, my teacher threatened me with detention for being tardy. It caused me to ask for my own alarm clock, and it caused me to always think I'd get in big trouble for being late … even a few minutes. Therefore, the shoe fits—I am a precrastinator.

Fears not dealt with accumulate over time. Think back to when you were in gym class at school and you were picked last for every team sport. That can lead to a fear of rejection as an adult, putting a serious cramp on any long-term relationships. Or perhaps you fear falling short of the expectations of others, causing you to constantly think you are a failure in the eyes of others. Or the opposite—fear of success. *What if I really succeed? What is that going to cost me? Will I then be living in a "glass house"? Will it change the dynamics of my relationships with those I care about?*

Or perhaps you have felt the fear of messing up so badly that God won't forgive me or be able to use me. Women, more than men, seem to deal with this fear deep within their souls. Let me speak to this for a moment. If you feel God won't use you because of the mess you've made of your life, you only have to look into Scripture to see this is not true. Those God used to deliver His people would never be picked as the "most likely to succeed in ministry," to put it mildly. Moses was a murderer. David, an adulterer and murderer. Peter denied Jesus three times. Paul dragged Christians from their homes to be tortured and killed.

NEVER LET FEAR KEEP YOU FROM BEING THE LEADER GOD HAS CALLED YOU TO BE. THE ENEMY WILL USE FEAR TO KEEP YOU TIED TO THE DOCK INSTEAD OF SAILING IN THE OCEAN OF GOD'S GRACE.

Do not let fear—any kind of fear—keep you from being the leader God has called you to be. The enemy will use fear to keep you tied to the dock instead of sailing in the ocean of God's grace, mercy, provision, and fulfillment for all your needs. Even the greatest fear of all—the fear of the unknown—gives way when we give God entrance to the deepest part of our lives. I found this out when I was diagnosed with cancer.

I was twenty-three years old and seven months pregnant with our first son. It was a Saturday, and I had talked Joe into going with me to a craft fair to find things for the nursery we were preparing. As we were returning home from the fair, having successfully finding exactly what I was looking for our baby's nursery, I reached up to scratch my neck and felt a lump that had not been there the day before. I knew immediately it wasn't supposed to be there. A few weeks of testing and then a biopsy confirmed the diagnosis I feared most. When my doctor spoke the "C" word to me—cancer—I was greatly tempted to give in to fear and shut myself off to the world, waiting for the end to come. But God, through His grace, saw me through. I never missed a Sunday leading worship at our church. I continued to lead the youth ministry, alongside Joe, and to go into the office every day. I'm not saying I was never afraid during this time, but I did not let fear take up residence in me. I did not know what the future held for me, but I knew the One who held me in His hand and would not let me go, no matter what.

Then there was the planting of Celebration Church, our church in Austin. The Lord spoke to Joe and me, separately and clearly, that we were to leave Louisiana, move to Austin, and start a church. That was all well and fine, except I had no idea where Austin was. But we were going where God called us regardless of where it was. We put a For Sale sign in our yard, packed our car, and loaded our three sons—at the time ages eight, four, and eight months old, and of absolutely no help whatsoever to us in the move—drove to Austin (I looked it up on the map), and bought a house before ours sold. At the time, wait-lists for apartments or rentals were at least six months, so we had no other choice. Then we searched for a place to meet as a church, settling on a public library in the North Austin suburb of Round Rock. We were living on our savings accounts and credit cards while trying to start a church from scratch. Were we afraid we might fail? To be honest, I don't think we had time to be afraid. But when we were tempted to fear, we confessed that God had called us to Austin, and He would never leave us nor forsake us.

One more story about a man tempted to fear. I mentioned Peter, the one Jesus appointed to lead His Church after Jesus ascended to the Father. We see Peter in the Gospels go from fear to failure to faith and back to fear again. There was the night when Jesus had instructed the disciples to cross the Sea of Galilee while He went up a mountain to pray. In the middle of the night a violent storm arose, and these men—for whom the sea was their second home—feared for their lives. The sea—which is really a very large lake—was eight miles across. These men were in the middle of the lake when the storm hit. Isn't that like our lives? We start well, and we finish well. It is the middle that brings us trouble. We have to go through the middle of our task, our trial, our life, if we are to reach the shore Jesus directs us toward. And the middle is often when it gets very dark, and we wonder if we really heard Jesus or not. We fear we may have just made the whole thing up in our heads, have taken a wrong turn somewhere. We think, *Surely, Jesus would not lead us right into the heart of a storm that could kill us.*

And yet Jesus does call us to pass through storms. In the book of Isaiah we read,

> *When you go through deep waters,*
>   *I will be with you.*
> *When you go through rivers of difficulty,*
>   *you will not drown.*
> *When you walk through the fire of oppression,*
>   *you will not be burned up;*
>   *the flames will not consume you.*

For I am the LORD, your God,
 the Holy One of Israel, your Savior....

Isaiah 43:2-3 (NLT)

Notice that Isaiah writes *when*, not *if*. We will go through deep waters, rivers of difficulty and the fire of oppression, yet we will not drown nor burn up. Why? *For I am the LORD, your God, the Holy One of Israel, your Savior.*

Back to the disciples in their boat. In the darkest part of that dark night, they spied what looked like a man walking on the water toward them. "It is a ghost!" they cried in terror.

"I'm not a ghost," said the man, who they now recognized as Jesus—or at least something that looked like Jesus. In all of their years of plying their trade as fishermen, they had never seen anyone walk on water, so they were very afraid, even more afraid of this water-walker than they were of the storm. Isn't that how God often comes to us—in a totally unexpected and mysterious manner? We are afraid of His approach, fearing it might be a spirit trying to impersonate the Lord. We don't want to step out in faith lest we be wrong and we sink beneath the waves. Jesus knows our fears. He responds to us as He did to His followers in their boat that night.

"Take courage, it is I; do not be afraid." (See Matthew 14 NASB for this whole story.)

Courage. This is a trait all women leaders must acquire. We must face each day with courage in order to carry out our commission from the Lord. You need courage to lead your children in today's culture. You need courage to lead your business in times of financial hardship. I needed courage to start a church out of nothing

YOU LACK NOTHING WHEN THE SPIRIT OF GOD IS WITH YOU.

in a city I'd never been to, and I still do to answer the demands of a growing ministry.

We develop courage in our souls as we focus on Jesus' words, "I am here." He was not just speaking of being "here" in the middle of the lake. He was speaking out who He is: I AM. He was declaring that He is the Great I AM, just as God declared to Moses in the midst of the burning bush. Do you fear what will happen in a close relation-ship? Jesus says I AM. Do you fear having to speak in public to share your story? Jesus is the Great I AM. Do you lack courage to be the leader you know God is calling you to be? God says I AM. There is nothing lacking when the Spirit of God is with you. And He is with all who call on the name of the Lord. If you have called on Jesus to forgive your sins and to be with you in this life in order that you can be with Him in the next, then the Great I AM dwells within you, and there will be no shortage nor lack. You can *Courage Up* because I AM is with you.

That does not mean you will not have times of fear. Peter, before starting out for the other side of the lake, had just witnessed a great miracle, the feeding of 5,000 people with just a couple of fish and a few loaves of bread. He and the other disciples even got to participate in the miracle as they obeyed Jesus and, through faith, gave the food to the crowd and then gathered up more leftovers than they could have eaten in a week. Peter was probably thinking, *We saw Jesus do a miracle and were able to do it with Him. Now He's doing another miracle—walking on water—and I want to do this with Him, too.*

GOD'S COMMAND +

OUR OBEDIENCE =

THE MIRACULOUS.

"Lord," he shouted above the wind and rain, "if it really is you, let me walk on the water, too." The *New King James Version* says it like this: *"Lord, if it is You, command me to come to You on the water"* (Matthew 14:28). There is a spiritual equation that says where there is a command of God along with our obedience to the command, what follows is the miraculous.

The command of God plus our obedience to God equals the miraculous. Jesus spoke one word to Peter: "Come!" And Peter obeyed this command. That's when we see the miracle.

I love Peter because he threw caution to the wind, went over the side of the boat, and started walking toward Jesus. His eyes were on the Lord, and his faith was in the Great I AM. That's when we see the frail faith and the failure Peter exhibited in this circumstance.

But when he saw that the wind was boisterous, he was afraid; and beginning to sink he cried out, saying, "Lord, save me!" (Matthew 14:30 NKJV).

Do you see the first word in that verse? *But.* Let me share a great revelation with you. Sometimes our big *buts* get in the way of a bigger God. *But.* Here Peter is walking on the water. *But* the wind. *But* the waves. How often we are like Peter. "But you don't know my situation—it's different than anyone else's situation. But you don't know how much pain I'm in. But you don't know how many bills we have that we can't pay." We let our big buts keep us from looking at Jesus who has called us to come to Him on the waves. He empowers us to walk to Him in the middle of the storm, yet we let our eyes focus on the boisterous wind and we become afraid.

One merit we must credit to Peter: He had the forethought to cry out, "Lord, save me!" This is the best prayer we can ever pray. Lord, save me. Save me in the midst of my storm, my fear, my failure. Sometimes God will still the storms that threaten to sink us. Sometimes God gives you peace while facing a storm. And sometimes He will call you to bravely walk to Him while the storm continues to surge.

Jesus grabbed Peter's hand and helped him get back into the boat. Then He spoke to Peter something that troubled me for quite a while.

He said, "Peter, you have so little faith. Why did you doubt Me?" Why does Jesus direct this to Peter when it should have been said to the other eleven who stayed in the boat? After all, Peter at least got out of the boat and took a few steps toward Jesus. But now I think I see what Jesus was saying to Peter. He was asking, "Where is the faith that sees you through? Where is the faith that gives you endurance? Where is the faith that doesn't just get you through easy times, but keeps you going in the hard times, the violent storms that you think will take you under?"

This tells me that we are not made by God to doubt in the middle of a miraculous event. When you are in the middle of a miracle it is not the time to quit. Jesus says that those who endure to the end will be saved. (See Matthew 24:13.) And endurance takes courage. My sister, now is the time to commit to Courage Up so that you can continue to obey Jesus' call to come to Him!

CHAPTER 5

WAKE UP

My zeal for God and his work burns hot within me....
Psalm 69:9 (TLB)

"And one day she discovered that she was fierce, and strong, and full of fire, and that not even she could hold herself back because her passion burned brighter than her fears."

—Mark Anthony

Our family is a very competitive family. *Very* competitive. My husband, Joe, played football for Louisiana State University. His father played and coached in the NFL for many years. Our three boys all played sports while growing up, with our middle son, Connor, now working as a college football coach. It's not just sports teams. We debate politics, social issues, opinions about who is best at what. We argue just for sport! It pushes each of us to be the best we can be. And we all play to win.

As I look at my family, full of strong (and very loud) opinionated people, one thing stands out to me from each of my boys (including

Joe) and now even my very strong daughter-in-law, Caroline: They have incredible passion in all they do. Everything they do is done with passion. Passion for life is what keeps them going through good times and bad. Most of all, their passion for Jesus, a great desire to know Him in greater ways every day, is the overarching motive in all that they do.

As for me, I grew up following in the wake of those who were very passionate for Jesus. My father lived to preach and to serve in the name of Jesus. He passed away while preaching in the church he and my mother started. After some years, my mother remarried a missionary and set out in the mission field when she was in her forties. She and her husband planted a church while in their fifties. My grandparents and great-grandparents all lived passionately for Jesus—maybe even a little *too* passionately at times (or some would say legalistic), but all motivated by a pure desire to please God in everything they did. That is my legacy—to live every day to make a difference in the life of God's most valued gift: people.

My mom has an old 8mm film (the kind you have to thread into a projector and watch on a screen or blank wall in your living room) of me when I was two or three years old. I was kneeling at a child-size wicker chair, crying "Jesus, Jesus, Jesus!" and totally unaware that Mom was filming me. I have a beautiful legacy of passion for Christ from my youngest days until now. Some might confuse tenacious passion for bossiness. But I agree with comedian Amy Poehler who said, "To me, bossy is not a pejorative term at all. It means somebody's passionate and engaged and ambitious and doesn't mind leading."

This was evident during my teenage years, especially at church. I would get all of my friends together in a pew and give them a pep talk before the service began.

"Okay, listen up. When the music starts, I want every single one of you clapping. You all are going to clap today. And lift your hands up to God, because He desires us to lift up holy hands to Him. And I want you to bounce a little. It will do you good to bounce."

Each week I would coach them how to passionately praise the Lord, encouraging them and instructing them how they could do it better. I was a passionate, crazy, nerdy worshipper in God's house, and I wanted everyone else to be like me in praising God.

Now I am leading my family to passionately follow and worship Jesus. As a family, we love watching football. We love talking politics and current events. We love traveling. We love our hobbies. But I am always there reminding us all that our greatest love, our most energetic efforts, are to be for the house of God and following His purpose for our lives. We all sacrifice for what is most important to us. We may say God is first, but what does that look like in our calendars and in our bank accounts? Our kids are watching what is most important to us, and that is reflected in how we allocate our time, our conversations, our money, and our personal devotion. They never woke up on a Sunday and wondered, "Are we going to church or are we going to the ballpark today?" *As for me and my house, we serve the Lord.* My kids knew that meant we orbited around God's house, even if they weren't able to join every extracurricular activity they wanted. Our kids knew that we wouldn't make a big decision without prayer and counsel from other godly people. Most importantly, our kids knew that we would take risks to pursue the call of God for our lives. We don't live "safe lives." Now they are young adults, and they are doing the same thing, risking, stepping out of their comfort zones, and passionately pursuing His will for their lives. The safest place you can ever be (even if it's in a persecuted mission field) is smack-dab in the middle of the perfect will of God.

MISPLACED PASSION

It was a hot day in May when we loaded up our three "non-morning people" children to drive two hours to Six Flags Fiesta Texas in

San Antonio for some forced fun. My thought was, if we were paying all that money, I wanted to make sure we were the first in line for the rides so we could make good use of our time. I began seeing a day at an amusement park as a contact sport, and I was pumped up to win.

A local high school senior class had the same idea, but they set out to accomplish that goal in a different way. As we waited at the opening gates behind just a handful of people who'd gotten there before us, I noticed that a few at a time, these red-shirted kids would come up to "talk to" someone ahead of us and then they'd just stay. Stay in front of us. Not behind us where the majority of their class-mates stood. Behind us there were probably twenty families that separated us and hundreds of kids from the class of 2007, where they should have been. But then there was this handful of sly kids wanting to get ahead of me and my family.

If there's something that sets me off, it's line-cutters. I've found myself in many conflicts over this issue. If you've ever been on an international flight, you'll know that people don't just file out row by row. In many countries they rush to the front of the plane, like a hijack scene is about to take place. That's just how it's done in other places. I have always had a problem with this—mostly because these people who were behind me for the whole flight were now in front of me to get off.

Meanwhile, back in Texas ... I watched as these kids continued to advance in the line, taking over those other helpless families who'd had crazy mornings like mine, trying to get their little ones out the door for a family day. I started (so the aggressors could hear me) loudly saying to my family, "They better not cut in front of us! I may have to get security!" It didn't help. Then I said, "Joe, kids, spread out, man your territory."

My kids and husband know this side of me, the side that goes a little crazy when someone tries to cut in line. I have a strong sense of justice, and I feel it's not right for people to cut in front of people who sacrificed to arrive early. Next thing you know, I look over and the high school kids had pulled even with us. I couldn't help myself. At that moment, I didn't care that we were outnumbered. I didn't care that we were pastors. I couldn't keep it in. I yelled, "Back yourself up! You are not getting in front of us!" I think I scared them right back to the back of the line.

Oh, my passion was set to overdrive that day.

And while passion for justice is right and good, passion can be misplaced or misused. Sometimes—including this day at Six Flags—I've spent my energy, passion, and even my outrage on the wrong things. Instead of making sure other amusement park enthusiasts stayed behind me, I sensed God asking me, "How about using that tenacity to worship Me? To serve others in My name? To ensure that your past stays behind you?"

DO NOT WORRY ABOUT FITTING IN WHEN YOU ARE SUPPOSED TO STAND OUT.

Where are your passions misguided? What bandwagon have you hopped on that you need to jump out of, even at the risk of skinning your knees? Let's not be so worried about fitting in when we are supposed to stand out. Let's not get so worked up over fighting to hold our place in the line we can't see we might be in the wrong line. Maybe instead of kicking people off the metaphoric corporate ladder we are trying to manhandle, we reach down and do the unthinkable, in our self-centered culture, we help someone else go up. Instead of plotting revenge (even if it's only in our heads) for the way we were looked over for that promotion, let's see that God's not freaking out. He's got an adventure down a road less traveled that He can't wait to show us. Author Hunter S. Thompson said he didn't want a safe arrival to his grave, but rather "to skid in broadside in a cloud of smoke, thoroughly used up, totally worn out, and loudly proclaiming, 'Wow! What a ride!'" Now that's the mark of a proper passionate life.

A GIFT FROM THE HOLY SPIRIT

True passion that leads us to bring glory to God is a gift of the Holy Spirt. Yet while it is begun by the Spirit, we are responsible to fan the flames. We do—and must—lead ourselves to the throne of God to give Him worship. We worship when we don't feel like it. We pray when we don't feel "spiritual." We devote ourselves to the Word as an act of faith before the feelings show up. It's less about emotion and more about decision. I don't always "feel" in love with my husband, but I love him nonetheless. Love is an ethic. Love is a commitment. The Bible says, "We bring a sacrifice of praise." That doesn't mean, "Look at me, I sang at church even though I had PMS." It means when I've been through the worst situation, the biggest disappointment, an unexpected diagnosis or job loss ... when the enemy has done his best to diminish the goodness of God in my life, *Yet will I praise Him.* Yet will I pursue Him with all my heart, as though I feel the passion, until I do feel the passion. David said, *"Restore unto me the joy of thy salvation."* He was in a tough season of life, yet he hadn't lost hope that his passion for God, and his gratefulness for God's salvation would be revived.

Real passion sometimes needs a wakeup call. There are many verses in God's Word that speak of our waking up passion for God. Here are just a few.

- *Awake, awake, clothe yourself in your strength, O Zion; Clothe yourself in your beautiful garments, O Jerusalem...* (Isaiah 52:1 NASB).

- *Awake, O my soul, with the music of his splendor-song! Arise, my soul, and sing his praises! My worship will awaken the dawn, greeting the daybreak with my songs of praise!* (Psalm 57:8 TPT).

- *How long do you plan to lounge your life away, you lazy fool? Will you ever get out of bed?* (Proverbs 6:9 The Voice).

- *Awake, O sleeper, rise up from the dead, and Christ will give you light* (Ephesians 5:14 NLT).

- *Wake up, Deborah, wake up! Wake up, wake up, and sing a song!...* (Judges 5:12 NLT).

Let's look at that last verse which speaks about our model female leader, Deborah. This may seem a little strange at first. After all, wasn't Deborah already awake? Wasn't it Deborah who woke up Barak and, thus, the armies of Israel? Let's look at another translation of this verse, the *Good News Translation*. There we read, *"Lead on, Deborah, lead on! Lead on! Sing a song! Lead on!"* Before we can be the leaders God calls us to be, we must wake up. And as we lead, we are singing a song to the Lord.

Just how do we wake up? Where does the passion to lead joyfully come from? This only comes as a gift from the Holy Spirit. It is our responsibility to wake up, to see that we are lacking passion, to see that we have strayed from passionately worshipping and serving the Lord. Once we are awake, it is the work of the Holy Spirit to build a fire within us that will last. But how do we wake up? Please tell me you are not one of those peppy morning people that I hate ... just kidding, I love you ... well, I love you after 10 a.m. Anyway, we are the ones in control of when we wake up and how we identify the places we are lacking to become fully motivated for our day. Do you go right to the shower? Do you work out? Or maybe have a cup ... or two ... or three ... of coffee to wake up? We all have things we do to wake up our bodies, but in the verses above, the Lord is exhorting us to wake up our *souls*. Try declaring this from Psalm 118:24 before you even get out of bed: "This is the day the Lord has made, and I will rejoice in all of His creativity." Waking our souls means continually turning to the Lord and taking His direction in all of your activities and decisions throughout the day.

In doing this, you will find that there are areas of your life you are keeping from the Lord. Or you may find that where the Holy Spirit used to speak clearly to you, His voice is now just a faint whisper. Listen, when we were saved, we were filled with God's Spirit. And yet we are leaky vessels. We need to continually be refilled with the oil of the Holy Spirit. Paul writes to the Ephesians, *"Be filled with the Spirit."* The unique structure of this sentence in Greek makes it read, "Be filled over and over with the Spirit." The Lord knows our nature, how we need the oil He fills us with, so He tells us to keep coming back for more. It is our responsibility to wake up and come to the Lord. It the responsibility of the Spirit of the Lord to fill us with His oil.

When my dad died, I felt nothing. Nothing. I was empty. That passionate girl who loved to worship the Lord had nothing to give. The girl I saw in the mirror didn't smile with her whole face. She smiled with her mouth, but her eyes were hollow. Then I remembered the times I had at Christian youth camp, those really special times where I got away in the presence of the Lord, and where spiritual memories were made that I could never forget. This is one of the places where I developed a very deep, very solid, very real experience with God. I remember being at the altar in the church at this camp, crying out to God, feeling like no one else was in the room. It was just me and the Lord. As I remembered these times, I woke up to find myself devoid of any sense of the God I loved.

I had lost my oil.

I kept going to church even though I still didn't feel like it. I told my friends, "I'm going to worship God as though I feel Him, even though I don't. I feel like my prayers don't rise above the ceiling, but I'm going to pray like God is listening anyway." I decided to walk in faith, acting as though God was still there, yet still wondering if He would come through for me. I did this for many weeks with no change in how I felt, with no breakthrough, always wondering when I would feel the wonderful presence of the Lord again.

One Sunday, six months after my dad died, I walked into a church I had never been to in my life. They opened with a few songs, and then someone preached. I really don't remember much of anything about the service. My focus was on getting to the altar. After the sermon, the pastor opened the altar for all those who desired prayer. I almost ran to the front of the church, straight to a prayer partner who asked how he could pray for me.

"I haven't felt a thing since my dad died," I said. "I haven't laughed. I haven't cried. I feel nothing."

As this man prayed for me, I began to feel once again. Tears streamed from my eyes, and the heaviness that had weighed me down began to lift. It was a feeling of freedom. I had tried to worship and pray, but it took the working of the Holy Spirit to set me free and fill me once again. I needed not only to feel, but to once again be passionate. Through this unknown man's kindness and prayer, the Holy Spirit released an even greater passion in my soul than I had ever known before.

SHOWING UP WILL WAKE YOU UP.

The Lord wants passionate leaders— passionate leaders in homes, in churches, in neighborhoods, in schools, in businesses. Yet for you to be a passionate leader, you must be passionate in your following of Jesus. The most passionate thing you can do sometimes is to keep showing up to church, to small group, to your time with the Lord, even when you least feel like it. My sister, it's amazing how showing up will eventually wake you up.

CHAPTER 6

RISE UP

Arise, shine, for your light has come, and the glory of the LORD
has risen upon you. For behold, darkness shall cover the earth,
and thick darkness the peoples; but the LORD will arise upon you,
and his glory will be seen upon you. And nations shall come
to your light, and kings to the brightness of your rising.

Isaiah 60:1-3

"The most beautiful people we have known are those who
have known defeat, known suffering, known struggle,
known loss and have found their way out of the depths.
These persons have an appreciation, a sensitivity and an
understanding of life that fills them with compassion, gentleness
and a deep loving concern. Beautiful people do not just happen."

—Elisabeth Kubler-Ross

When I do sickness, I do it big.

I had worked all day at the church, and throughout the day was
bugged by pain in the area of my right kidney. I wasn't too worried as

I had previously endured kidney stones which, while very painful, did not keep me down for very long. Yet this time, I felt increasingly worse until by evening I could only lie on the couch. I was nauseated and running a slight fever. Finally, I asked Joe to take me to the hospital.

Once I was in an emergency room cubicle, the doctor came in to exam me. I immediately recognized the name on her badge, just as she greeted me by name, surprised to see me at the hospital. Earlier that day, I'd opened a gift in my office and had searched social media to try to put a face with the name on the card. It turned out to be this doctor. While I didn't know her, she attended our church, and was thoughtful enough to bring me some souvenirs (including chocolates) from her recent trip to Europe. I immediately felt that the timing wasn't coincidental, that God was at work and I was in good hands. Yet I didn't feel very much like socializing, as the pain, fever, and nausea kept me from really being able to focus on anything at that moment.

"Lori, I can see you are in real pain," she said. "I'm going to get a CT scan right away, and then I'll be back to see you." A few minutes later, an x-ray technician arrived to take me to the imaging center where they did a CT scan and then wheeled me back to my cubicle. The doctor came in once again and said, "Lori, you have a significant kidney infection. It has overtaken your whole kidney. You do have a stone, but I believe your pain is coming from the infection and the fever caused by the infection. A urologist will need to operate and place a stent in the kidney to keep it from shutting down entirely."

The doctor told me what to expect before, during and after the operation, which she said would only take about ten minutes. I barely heard her—I was really "out of it." And poor Joe—it was by now the middle of the night, and he was so tired. He could barely speak, but did pray a very brief prayer as I was being taken to the OR. "Bless her, Lord," is all I remember him saying.

The first thing I saw when I woke in the recovery room was a whole team of people gathered around me. "Oh, Lori," cried the respiratory therapist (who introduced herself as a Celebration Church member), and then she reached down and hugged me. The others there seemed to be anxious and worried. They quickly took me to ICU where I was hooked up to various machines and monitors. In a few minutes the urologist who did the surgery came into my room,

"We almost lost you," he said. "Your blood pressure dropped to 50 over 30. You were in septic shock."

Later I found out that septic shock is often fatal, killing more than a quarter of a million people in the United States every year. It occurs when there is a major infection in the body, causing the blood pressure to drop dramatically. This, in turn, leads to vital organs in the body shutting down, which leads to death.

This is not what I had in my planner for that week!

Following this crisis, I was in the hospital for six days. When I was discharged, it was to home and bed rest. I was to avoid being around crowds of people for several weeks until my immune system regained strength. So, it was a very big moment for me when I was able to return to church. I was really looking forward to our Saturday night service.

But before that time arrived, I found myself struggling under what felt like the weight of the world on my back.

A DREAM—AND A NIGHTMARE

Friday morning, I was in that fuzzy place between being asleep and awake when dreams can be very strong and memorable. The dream I had early that morning found me in church leading during the Prayer and Welcome time. At Celebration Church, we have a time when a member of the pastoral staff comes forward to share a brief reflection on a Scripture passage, a testimony or word of encouragement, leading to a time of corporate prayer for general needs in the congregation. We call it "Prayer and Welcome." You might think I do this all the time, that I love being in the spotlight with a microphone in my hand. In reality, nothing could be further from the truth. I am actually much happier to have others in that role. In fact, I've had two panic attacks in my life and both happened while ministering on stage. Since then, I have had to be pushed, prodded, and poked in order to get me in front of an audience. Yet in my dream I was at peace, knowing God was with me in the sharing time.

I finally woke all the way and began my day. Joe was going to be out of town that weekend, honoring a speaking engagement in Georgia. As he was packing on Friday, he turned to me and said, "You are supposed to do prayer and welcome this weekend." I immediately thought of my dream of doing prayer and welcome, and excitement began to build in my soul. Yet at the same time I began to be afraid. I had not done this in a long time, and I didn't feel I was in a healthy emotional state to re-enter ministering in public.

"I'm not sure I can do it," I said.

"No, you're supposed to do it," said my husband. "As a matter of fact, I'm going to send out a tweet right now to let people know they need to be there this weekend to hear you."

"Oh, no! Please don't do that," I said. "That will make me too nervous."

"I'm going to send that tweet, and I'm going to let the staff know you are doing the Prayer and Welcome time this weekend. I know you'll do a great job."

Yes, I am a leader. Yes, I can be bossy. Yes, I see myself as a strong woman who takes charge and shows the way to go to both women and men. But I am also a wife who is in submission to her husband just as we are taught to be in Scripture. I have always prayed for my husband to hear from God and to lead according to what he hears.

Since I pray that, how can I reject what he says I am to do, even if it causes fear in my heart? I agreed to do as he asked that weekend.

Very early on Saturday morning as I was still asleep, Joe came into the bedroom with a clatter. He said, "Lori, have you seen my iPad with my sermon notes on it? I can't find it." Before I could respond, he added, "Oh, and Ed died."

Ed died. He said it just like that. I was now fully awake, but with a heaviness and sadness approaching what I felt when my dad died.

Ed Werner was my dad's best friend and a trustee of my father's church as well as Celebration Church. The man who stepped in as a father figure for my brothers and me. The man my kids knew as "Gran." Ed was our biggest cheerleader when we left Louisiana to plant a church in Austin, Texas. We knew he was in the hospital being treated for a blood clot, but we had heard he was recovering and would be home soon. And now to be told he had died, all mixed in with a search for a missing iPad, left me speechless.

"Oh, Lori—I'm sorry," said my husband. He came over and hugged me, saying, "I know how very much he meant to you, to both of us. I'm so sorry."

After he left, I did something I very seldom do: I cried. I wept huge tears and wailed. When someone who does not typically cry begins to cry, tears come out for all that should have been cried over for many years. That Saturday it all gushed forth. By noon, I was a complete wreck. I had a text conversation with Joe that went like this.

Me: I don't know if I can minister tonight. I'm a wreck. I wanted to walk up strong and confident.

Joe: You will be by tonight. You can do this. You need to do it.

Me: Please don't make me do this.

Joe: If Ed were here, he would say, "You got this, girl."

Me: That's the problem. Ed isn't here.

A couple of hours later, I texted him again.

Me: I can't stop sobbing … It's been a hard few weeks and I'm feeling devastated.

Joe: I agree … I'm so sorry.

I was weighed down with grief and anger, not to mention just being a few weeks removed from nearly dying. Gravity firmly had me in its grip.

THE STRENGTH OF GRAVITY

Gravity is a universal force that causes matter (that is, every created thing) to be pulled toward one another. And the bigger the matter, the more gravity it exerts. The biggest physical matter where you and I live is, of course, the Earth. That's why when you drop a glass, it crashes to the floor instead of smacking you in the forehead.

There is gravity in the physical world, and there is gravity in the spiritual world. Just as in the physical world, gravity is dependent on weight—the greater the weight of an object, the greater its gravitation pull—so it is with spiritual gravity. Spiritual gravity comes from what we give weight to in our souls. Do you give weight to words spoken in anger or judgment by others? Do you give weight to fears and failures? The writer of the book of Hebrews tells us, *"Therefore, since we are surrounded by so great a cloud of witnesses, let us also lay aside every weight, and sin which clings so closely, and let us run with endurance the race that is set before us"* (Hebrews 12:1). We are all in a race, and in order to win, we need to shed those things weighing us down. As leaders, we cannot let spiritual gravity hold us down. We must strive to get rid of weights that may prevent us from winning. We need to fight against the deadly pull of negative spiritual gravity. And we need to lead others in this as well. I want to share three things we need to do in order to be *anti-gravity* leaders.

BEYOND LIMITATIONS

The first thing an anti-gravity leader must do is look beyond limitations. We all have aspects of our lives that we think will limit us in our ability to lead. Perhaps the biggest is the fear of failure. We don't want others to believe we are incompetent in our roles. For many, the fear of failure keeps them from moving forward. After all, if we don't try, we won't fail, right?

Let's consider one of the world's greatest "failures": Peter. We already saw him take a few steps on the water, then look down and sink beneath the waves. We also see him make a Spirit-led confession of who Jesus truly is—the Messiah, the Anointed One of God—and then hear Jesus rebuke Peter for saying He shouldn't talk about going to His death. We watch Peter, along with James and John, go up a hill with Jesus where Moses and Elijah appear to discuss with the Messiah the trial that awaits Him. Peter, overcome with emotion and passion, cries out, "This is great, Jesus! Moses and Elijah here with us. Let's put up three tents for you all to stay in." This time the rebuke comes verbally from God the Father, speaking from a cloud, *"This is my beloved Son. Listen to Him."*

Peter messed up at every turn, and yet it was he who Jesus picked to be a leader in His Church. The other disciples were equally unqualified as theologians, strategic planners, or world-class scholars, and yet they went throughout the then-known world proclaiming the Good News. Fear of failing did not keep them from leading as the Lord called them to do.

Paul (another great failure—before his conversion, he sought out Christians to have them killed) wrote something that, on the face of it, makes no sense. He told the church at Corinth what Jesus told him: *"My grace is sufficient for you, for my power is made perfect in weakness..."* (2 Corinthians 12:9). In today's world, that's crazy talk! How many have delighted in weaknesses lately? Have you delighted in insults, in hardships, in persecutions, in difficulties? Anti-gravity leaders push beyond their own weaknesses to be covered in Jesus' power. Anti-gravity leaders don't hide from their shortcomings, their failures, their incompetence. Instead, they rejoice in these, knowing that the power of Jesus will then be evident in their lives.

Our "buts" often weigh us down, keeping us from pushing forward. We've all heard of the famous *Footprints in the Sand* poem, a beautiful picture of how God carries us through difficulties. But there's a new comedic and often more accurate version, called *Butt-prints in the Sand*. We see a picture of how "buts" became limitations for the nation of Israel. The Hebrews had been wandering in the wilderness for forty years when Moses sent twelve men—one from each tribe of Israel—to spy out the Promised Land. These men (we read their story in the book of Numbers, chapter 13) came back with stories of abundance in that land. They even brought back evidence in the form of bunches of grapes so big they had to be carried by two of the men on a pole. But. "But there are giants in that land," said ten of the men. "There is no way we can conquer them." They did not figure on the power of God who had given them the land to conquer. They put limitations on what could be done with their "buts." Fortunately, there were two of the spies who pushed beyond these limitations, and these two (Joshua and Caleb) became anti-gravity leaders and encouraged the Hebrews on to victory in the Promised Land. They did not let the gravity keep them back, but instead acted on the words Moses spoke to them.

"GOD will lavish you with good things: children from your womb, offspring from your animals, and crops from your land, the land that GOD promised your ancestors that he would give you. GOD will throw open the doors of his sky vaults and pour rain on your land on schedule and bless the work you take in hand. You will lend to many nations but you yourself won't have to take out a loan. GOD will make you the head, not the tail; you'll always be the top dog, never the bottom dog, as you obediently listen to and diligently keep the commands

of GOD, *your God, that I am commanding you today"* (Deuteronomy 28:11-14 MSG).

Now that's an anti-gravity scripture!

PRESS THROUGH

Being an anti-gravity leader is hard. Gravity is a powerful force. Don't let anyone make you think it is easy, and don't think you're doing it wrong if things are going wrong. Perhaps you are doing things so right that you are being attacked for it. Don't quit. Obey the Lord. Press through the gravitation tug and break through to the place of freedom. In doing so, you will make a way for others who follow to be free as well.

Philippians 3:14 reads, *"I press on toward the goal for the prize of the upward call of God in Christ Jesus."* As we read the writings of Paul, we see that his life was no picnic. He faced constant opposition to his preaching, both from Jews and Gentiles. He was stoned and left for dead. He was shipwrecked on an island. He was imprisoned. He was hunted. Yet Paul did not let these circumstances keep him down. *"I press on."* We have to resist the temptation to give ourselves a pass when we are called on to lead (like I was called on to lead "Prayer and Welcome" in our church) just because leading is hard.

Pressing on does not mean just surviving. Determine you will gain ground as you push past the gravity trying to keep you down. Don't think of just "getting back to how I used to be." Don't make being comfortable your goal. It is most certainly *not* comfortable to press on through difficulties that threaten to take

GAIN GROUND AS YOU PUSH PAST THE GRAVITY TRYING TO KEEP YOU DOWN. ANTI-GRAVITY LEADERS ARE BOTH ALTITUDE AND ATTITUDE SHIFTERS.

you under. But as you do press on in learning to be an anti-gravity leader, you will find you are developing "spiritual muscles" that will help you to rise up against the gravity in your life.

SHIFT THE ALTITUDE AND ATTITUDE

The third characteristic of anti-gravity leaders is that they are both altitude and attitude shifters. They are those who brighten a room just by entering, who seek the positive rather than focusing on the negative in life. They are leaders in hope rather than purveyors of despair.

One of my favorite scriptures is found in Colossians. *"Christ in you, the hope of glory"* (Colossians 1:27). We have Jesus the Christ ("Christ" means Messiah, God's Anointed One) in us. He is the hope of glory. We can walk with hope because Jesus is Life—He gives us life, not death, as we walk with Him. Do you walk in hope in life? Do you scatter "life beams" wherever you go? If not, then I urge you to put yourself—your desires, your goals, your ego—to the back and let Jesus walk in you and for you. We must shift our attitude of ourselves if we are to raise the altitude of those around us, those we lead. Gathering women of faith and life around us to push us and help us to rise up against the gravity of this world is not just a good idea. We must have them with us to shift attitudes and altitudes.

PASSING THE TEST

Gravity surely had me in its grip the Saturday I lost Ed and was scheduled to minister. My eyes were chapped from all my crying. I felt like I was grasping for a lifeline to keep from going under. Then our women's ministries pastor, who is also one of my closest friends, called. I choked out what I was going through and what I was facing that evening. She said, "Well, since you've been there all day by yourself crying, I'm going to come over and do your hair and makeup."

(Sometimes the best ministry a girl can get is having someone do her hair and makeup.) I said okay, but told her it would be a challenge to get any makeup on my face after all of that. She managed to get me ready, even though I was still weeping.

She drove me to church, encouraging me with her words and her anti-gravity leadership ability. Her attitude raised my altitude. When the time came for me to minister, I went forward, heart beating out of my chest. When I walked across the stage, the church roared in cheers as they had carried me in prayer. I shared what I had been through the last few weeks. Then I shared about Ed Werner passing away. Our church knew Ed from what Joe and I had said about him, and from all of the times that he had come to visit. They knew he gave a sizeable donation to help start the church. I showed pictures of Ed in ministry, of Ed with our kids. I showed a picture of his wife worshipping by his hospital bed—it was the ultimate picture of an anti-gravity leader. I can't say I've ever had a more powerful time of ministry, where I felt the strength of the Lord more present. It was raw and emotional, but you are most relatable when leading from the place of vulnerability combined with God's presence. There's something about going against the current of gravity. There's something about ministering out of your own emptiness, and seeing God fill the void to overflowing, as only He can.

That evening I talked with my husband. He asked, "Was it good?"

I took a deep breath and said, "Yeah, it was good."

He smiled, knowingly, "I knew it would be."

CHAPTER 7

WISE UP

She conducts her conversations with wisdom, and
the teaching of kindness is ever her concern.

Proverbs 31:26 (The Voice)

"A strong woman understands that the gifts such as
logic, decisiveness, and strength are just as feminine
as intuition and emotional connection.
She values and uses all of her gifts."

—Nancy Rathburn

I love to teach from the Bible. Reading, studying, praying with and sharing God's Word energizes me. I get great joy when I can show other women how God wants us to live and work and act as leaders. No matter if it is a small Bible study or a filled-to-the-brim women's conference, give me a Bible and a room full of women hungry to learn and I will teach until I drop.

Yet as a young woman, I would have rather had a root canal without anesthesia than attend a class on biblical womanhood. I loved the Bible. I loved being a woman. But those two words mashed-up together looked to me the very opposite of what I was built for. God had gifted me with a strong mind for business, given me an entrepreneurial spirit, made me strong and strong-willed. The only way I saw to put these gifts to use was outside of the church. I could not see a role for a woman like me in the church. To me, women's ministries looked more like women's *miseries*, and I wanted no part of that.

I was familiar with what I heard referred to as the "Proverbs 31 Woman." As I said, I loved the Bible (still do!) and read it every day. But I avoided Proverbs 31. I imagined that the woman described in this chapter would be a woman wearing a lace-collared, drop-waist dress spending all her time quoting scriptures to her flock of nineteen kids (who she had given birth to at home). Or one of those women from 1960s black-and-white TV shows who wore a dress (along with a string of pearls) and heels as she swept the house, just waiting for her husband to get home so she could fetch him his pipe and slippers. No thank you. That wasn't for me.

And then one day I was liberated by the very chapter that I thought was put in the Bible to slap the hands of women like me. It turns out that the Proverbs 31 woman was way more multifaceted than I'd imagined. Yes, she was an incredible wife and mother, but she was respected outside of the home for her reach into the community and for her business savvy. You may have read this passage many times (unless you do like I did and skip right over it), but I want to present it to you in a different version than we are accustomed to hearing. In *The Message*, Proverbs 31:10-31, Eugene Peterson titles this passage, "Hymn to a Good Wife."

A good woman is hard to find,
and worth far more than diamonds.
Her husband trusts her without reserve,
and never has reason to regret it.

Never spiteful, she treats him generously
  all her life long.
She shops around for the best yarns and cottons,
  and enjoys knitting and sewing.
She's like a trading ship that sails to faraway places
  and brings back exotic surprises.
She's up before dawn, preparing breakfast
  for her family and organizing her day.
She looks over a field and buys it,
  then, with money she's put aside, plants a garden.
First thing in the morning, she dresses for work,
  rolls up her sleeves, eager to get started.
She senses the worth of her work,
  is in no hurry to call it quits for the day.
She's skilled in the crafts of home and hearth,
  diligent in homemaking.
She's quick to assist anyone in need,
  reaches out to help the poor.
She doesn't worry about her family when it snows;
  their winter clothes are all mended and ready to wear.
She makes her own clothing,
  and dresses in colorful linens and silks.
Her husband is greatly respected
  when he deliberates with the city fathers.
She designs gowns and sells them,
  brings the sweaters she knits to the dress shops.
Her clothes are well-made and elegant,
  and she always faces tomorrow with a smile.
When she speaks she has something worthwhile to say,
  and she always says it kindly.
She keeps an eye on everyone in her household,
  and keeps them all busy and productive.

Her children respect and bless her;
her husband joins in with words of praise:
"Many women have done wonderful things,
but you've outclassed them all!"
Charm can mislead and beauty soon fades.
The woman to be admired and praised
is the woman who lives in the Fear-of-God.
Give her everything she deserves!
Festoon her life with praises!

This is no weak little housewife. This is Wonder Woman! This is a multifaceted woman of strength, wisdom, and godliness. The fruit of her life is seen all around her; her husband, her kids, the community, and even the economy are lifted because of her. What she did to lift others privately has been shouted from the rooftops.

These days it's controversial to talk about the different roles of men and women. Our culture is extremely hostile to the uniqueness of the sexes. It tells us that just because you have a few different body parts, it doesn't mean that men and women aren't interchangeable. Gender is unimportant; therefore, you should no longer even refer to people using gender-specific pronouns. I saw one list that had eighty-nine different gender identity terms. This is a complete separation from God's view of His creation. Gender distinctiveness is God's; it is the way He designed us all. And God does not make mistakes. In Genesis we read, *"God created them male and female...."* Two genders, created equally in God's image, with different functions, different ways of expressing ourselves and emotions, different roles in bringing others into God's world.

We see more of this diversity as the Creation story unfolds in Genesis 2:18-25 (TLB).

And the Lord God said, "It isn't good for man to be alone; I will make a companion for him, a helper suited to his needs." So the Lord God formed from the soil every kind of animal and bird, and brought them to the man to see what he would call them; and whatever he called them, that was their name. But still there was no proper helper for the man. Then the Lord God caused the man to fall into a deep sleep, and took one of his ribs and closed up the place from which he had removed it, and made the rib into a woman, and brought her to the man.

"This is it!" Adam exclaimed. "She is part of my own bone and flesh! Her name is 'woman' because she was taken out of a man." This explains why a man leaves his father and mother and is joined to his wife in such a way that the two become one person. Now although the man and his wife were both naked, neither of them was embarrassed or ashamed.

God, as a relational God, made woman as a solution to the problem of aloneness. Man was created in the image of God, and even God needs the community of the Trinity. A triune God—Father, Son, Spirit—the same in substance, but different in function. Our Creator knew that Adam would not be complete if he were alone. He created Eve from Adam's side, and Adam called her woman. Or, more likely, he took one look at her and said, "Woe! Man!"

GOD MADE WOMAN AS A SOLUTION TO THE PROBLEM OF ALONENESS.

Eve was created from Adam to be his companion and his helper. This is where a lot of women struggle. Some think that being called a "helper" means that women are less than men. "Helper" isn't a very glamorous term. But if we look closely at that word, we will come away rejoicing to be called "helper."

In Hebrew, the word for "helper" used in Genesis chapter two, verses 18 and 20, is *ezer* (pronounced "ay-zer"). It is always used in the Old Testament in the context of vitally important and powerful acts of rescue and support. The word *ezer* is only used twenty-one times in the Old Testament. Twice it is used in the context of the first woman. Three times in a military context and sixteen times it is used in reference to God as a helper. *Ezer* describes aspects of God's character: He is our strength, our rescuer, our protector, and our help. And *ezer* was the Holy Spirit's word of choice to describe the first woman. Eve was someone who would provide valuable and vital strength to Adam.

The word *ezer* is qualified by the word *kenegdo* in both verses in Genesis chapter two regarding the woman. *Ezer* always refers to a strong type of help, a rescuer who risks all to save. *Kenegdo* is seen in the *King James Version* as the word "meet," as in "a helpmeet for him." This has been mistranslated by some as "helpmate." In reality, *kenegdo* means "fit for" or "corresponding to." Thus, we read *ezer kenegdo* as "power and strength fit for man." This shows that Eve was designed to be a complimentary and equal partner for Adam. There is no sense of subordination stated, implied, or even hinted at in this passage in Genesis.

All was well in the Garden as Adam and Eve learned their personal uniqueness, strengths and weaknesses, and learned to work together as equal but different persons. But then, something happened ...

"Now the serpent was more crafty (subtle, skilled in deceit) than any living creature of the field which the Lord God had made. And the serpent (Satan) said to the woman, "Can it really be that God has said, 'You shall not eat from any tree of the garden'?" Genesis 3:1 (AMP).

HER PROTECTOR BECAME HER ACCUSER.

Satan appealed to her, as a woman, through the ear-gate—through communication. Have you ever wondered how unattractive men can sometimes attract a beautiful woman? It's because, unlike men (who are stimulated by the eye), women can be drawn in by communication—that less than handsome guy probably has a "gift of gab" or at least the ability to charm with words. Satan appealed to Eve by saying, *"Your eyes will be opened … you will be like God"* (Genesis 3:5 AMP). She saw it was good food and delightful to look at—women are sense-driven. Eve stepped outside of the order of leadership that God had set in place with her husband and she went solo. You see, not only did Adam need Eve, but Eve needed Adam. Had she consulted with the one God had given to her as her husband, together they could've navigated this temptation and been victorious. But they both ended up sinning and thus losing their ability to reflect God.

The battle of the sexes began. When confronted by God, while hiding and covering their nakedness and asked if they'd eaten from the tree, Adam says, *"The woman whom You gave to be with me—she gave me [fruit] from the tree, and I ate it"* (Genesis 3:12 AMP). *She made me do it.*

Her protector became her accuser.

God didn't hesitate for one moment to provide their salvation, saying to the serpent that the seed of the woman (Jesus) would bruise his head, and he would bruise his (Jesus') heel. Adam then named his wife Eve which means "mother of all the living," or "life-giver." This means that women birth children, but it also means that every redeemed woman can be a life-giver in every relationship and every season of life. This is good news, the gospel, that even out of death, there can be life!

WE AREN'T TO LEAD AT THE EXPENSE OF MEN, BUT ALONGSIDE THEM.

Let's take another look at the story of Deborah. This story, for me as a leader working alongside not only my husband but also other men, fleshes out how a woman uniquely leads. We aren't to lead at the expense of men or in the place of men, but right alongside them, with our unique but equally valuable gifts. Deborah, as we read earlier, was a judge in Israel in very difficult times. The Jews had once again departed from the commands of God and were subjected to their enemies the Canaanites. For twenty long years the Jews were forced to do whatever Jabin, the king of the Canaanites, wanted them to do. Finally, they had had enough. They cried out to God, whom they had abandoned for earthly pleasures, and God heard them. The Lord spoke to the judge of Israel at this time, a woman named Deborah. The Lord said, "Call Barak to come see you. When he arrives, tell him that I have ordered him to raise an army of ten thousand men and muster them at Mount Tabor. I will draw Sisera, general of the Canaanite troops, there as well, and Barak's army will destroy Sisera's army."

Note that God did not speak directly to Barak; rather, he spoke to Barak through a woman. Also note that Barak respected Deborah and did just what she said. He also asked Deborah to go with him—as a matter of fact, he made her accompany him as a requirement for him gathering the army of the Lord to him to assemble.

Deborah had gained a reputation as a strong leader in Israel. She had great wisdom—Jews from all over would seek her to settle disputes and give direction for their lives. Deborah was not the Lone Ranger. She was married to Lappidoth, whose name means "torches" or "flames." It is said that Deborah encouraged her husband to make tall wicks for the oil lamps in the Tabernacle, thus drawing the people's attention back to the Torah—the teachings of Moses. Some Jewish scholars and teachers say that Lappidoth ("flames") and Barak (meaning "lights") are the same person, that God used Deborah to call her husband to raise an army to defeat Sisera.

While we can't know for certain if the two were the same man, we do know for sure that God called Deborah to show the people of Israel the way back to the Lord. She held court out in the open under a palm tree where all could see her. She was a leader in a very difficult time, a strong leader in a time of fear, uncertainty, and confusion.

I want to point out a few things that women who want to be used of God can learn from Deborah.

PROTECTOR

When I hear the word "protector," my thoughts don't immediately envision a woman. Honestly, I think of Mel Gibson in that famous Braveheart moment, shouting to his men in a selfless act of war, "Men don't follow titles, they follow courage!" Maybe that's because I live in an overly testosterone-filled house. But when I really think about it, it's one of our most instinctual gifts as women. I remember some bully making fun of my best friend. In that moment, no one was more protective, demonstrative, authoritative about setting that idiot straight than I was—no matter the cost. (If you can't tell, I'm a very loyal person.) And don't even get me started with motherhood. Nobody is going to mess with my babies! There's nothing more dangerous than a mama on a playground, watching like a hawk to make sure her child isn't pushed around.

In fact, God Himself shares this quality and compared Himself to a female when it comes to displaying His protective nature. *"How often would I have gathered your children together as a hen gathers her brood under her wings..."* (Matthew 23:37).

When it comes to Deborah, she was protective of the destiny of Israel and the will of God being accomplished. Even in her relationship with a strong man, Barak, she was never about exploiting his weaknesses or exposing his insecurities so that he wouldn't doubt as a result of being on the losing team of some previous battles.

IT'S NOT ABOUT COMPETITION, IT'S ABOUT COMPLETION.

It's not about competition. It's about completion. If we can come to grips with that truth, if we can operate

95

without a chip on our shoulder or without feeling the need to prove ourselves, we can actually win together. As President Harry Truman said, "It is amazing what you can accomplish if you do not care who gets the credit."

Women were taken from the rib. The function of the rib is to protect the vital organs of the body: the heart, the lungs, the breath, the life. Deborah was protective of the people under her care— protecting them from the enemies without and wrong beliefs within each of the Israelites. Who has God placed in your care? How are you working to protect them today?

UNCOMPLICATED

We read that while she was seated under the palm tree, *"the sons of Israel came up to her for judgment"* (Judges 4:5 NASB). Men will not willingly receive from complicated women who use a lot of words and emotions. They don't even like or read long text messages. Give them the bullet points. (I know this as I'm a mom of all boys, and a sister of all brothers, and someone who works with mostly men.) Deborah could have hard conversations without being harsh or dramatic.

As women, we are complex and multifaceted. That's not a bad trait—it's beautiful, like a masterfully-cut diamond. We don't have to be, nor should we be, "complicated." We should not be the ones that people have to walk on eggshells around. We should not be the ones having the meeting after the meeting in the office, where we don't speak up when everyone is in the room, but criticize what happened after the meeting is over. Godly women are not passive-aggressive or manipulative. They are simply honest. I desire to be around people who give wisdom (even when it's not what I want to hear, but what I need to hear), when there aren't hidden agendas. Uncomplicated.

STRATEGIC

She outlined the battle plans for Barak, not because of her military prowess, but because she knew how to hear from God. As women, I believe we are uniquely tuned into God and are given to focusing on details. In my function, I've been able to provide specific strategy and practicality to big visions because of how God made me to think.

As women, we are multitasking, complex-thinking geniuses, who have to use critical thinking skills not just in the workplace, but at home. Have you ever had to leave directions with a house/babysitter when going on an extended trip? When you write it all down, it's shocking how much we do without even thinking about it. We aren't just tactical, we are visionary and strategic.

SECURE

Deborah was secure and made sure she infused security into those around her. When Barak asked her to go with him, she said she would go, but that the glory of the victory would belong to a woman. She wasn't emasculating him in this statement; she was secure enough to be sensitive to his manhood. And because of her sensitivity, Barak was absolutely fine knowing that she might receive all of the credit.

Are people more or less secure when you are around? Are you waiting for people to mess up, or do you look for ways to highlight their wins, to build confidence in people? A Harvard research report showed that if your boss thinks you're doing great, you'll do even greater. The people who are led by secure leaders, who are infused with security and given positive feedback, actually become better at what they do.

SPEAK TO POTENTIAL, NOT TO POSTURE.

INSPIRATIONAL

She spoke to potential not to posture. This is one of the most life-giving things about this story. Barak had gathered the army as Deborah directed him. The day had come for battle. And yet Barak was sleeping in that morning. Deborah approached him and said, *"Up! For this is the day on which the LORD has given Sisera into your hand. The LORD is indeed going out before you"* (Judges 4:14 NRSV). I don't know why she had to tell Barak to get up. His army was ready, Sisera's army was ready. She'd already told him the plans and that victory was in his future. But she didn't belittle him, she didn't say, "Why do I have to tell you this again? Am I going to have to go into battle for you?" She just reminded him of the call of God on his life and that God had already gone before him.

We all know moms who believe their kids can do anything, whereas the dads may be a little more realistic in their views. I believe that God has graced us as women to use the gift of seeing potential in others to inspire people to do great things, to wake up potential in people who God has brought into our lives. We are atmosphere setters in our homes, in our church, in our communities.

Deborah was the embodiment of the Proverbs 31 woman. She was strong and yet sensitive to others. She was wise and willing to freely share that wisdom with others. She worked well with her husband to point people to the light of God's Truth. Most of all, she loved the Lord and led the way for others to follow in the ways of the Lord to gain the victory.

CHAPTER 8

TEAM UP

Two are better than one, because they have a good
return for their labor: If either of them falls down,
one can help the other up. But pity anyone who falls and
has no one to help them up. Also, if two lie down together,
they will keep warm. But how can one keep warm alone?

Ecclesiastes 4:9-11 (NIV)

"God designed husbands and wives to complete each other,
not to compete with each other."

—Unknown

I have some breaking news for you. It may come as a shock to you, so perhaps you should sit down and take a few deep, calming breaths before I tell you.

Ready?

Men and women are different.

There, the secret is now out. Men and women really are different from each other. Does that shock you? Based on what we hear in our culture—that men and women are interchangeable in every way—it may actually be breaking news for some. This is the cause of so much confusion and hurt, especially among our young people. Gender confusion isn't just seen in the pronoun someone wants to be called. It is seen daily in the workplace as women strive to be just like men instead of being the woman they were made to be.

My purpose in writing this book is to help you embrace who you are as a *woman* leader. Trying to become a manly leader is misspent time and effort. You cannot become a manly leader for one specific reason: You are not a man! Men who are leaders are not better than nor less than women who are leaders. Men and women are equally capable of being leaders, but there are distinct differences in how they fill that role. Each one brings different skills, abilities, strengths, and weaknesses to the task. And once we learn what those differences are, we can be who we truly are and lead as we were made to lead.

What's essential to note here is that both women and men have important skill areas in which they naturally excel. Relying primarily on the strength of just one gender as leaders can result in an imbalance of perspectives and ideas. On the other hand, when women and men work side by side on the leadership team and in the boardroom, this diversity of perspectives can lead to more innovative thinking. This better balance, in turn, can result in greater productivity, improved engagement, higher profits, and a sustainable competitive advantage.

Author Arianna Huffington says, "It would be futile to attempt to fit women into a masculine pattern of attitudes, skills and abilities and disastrous to force them to suppress their specifically female characteristics and abilities by keeping up the pretense that there are no differences between the sexes."

As a woman leader, you will often be called to lead men or co-lead with men. It is so important to understand the difference in leadership—and followership—in men and women. You need to be confident in who you are to keep from trying to be who you are not. Leading and teamwork requires you to know your strengths as well as areas of your life where you need to accept the help of others to accomplish what is before you. And because of the differences between men and women, we waste a lot of time trying to get others to be like we are rather than seeing the benefit of teaming with someone who is different from us. For instance, women have greater peripheral vision while men have greater long-distance sight. I can't tell you how many arguments my husband and I have had while we are driving somewhere. He is constantly asking me to check the GPS to see what is happening thirty miles down the road while we are going right by our exit. I have no idea how he gets anywhere when I'm not with him. Can't he check his own GPS? And while he could find his way out of a forest blindfolded, he can't find the butter in the 'fridge when it's right in front of his eyes!

Neither one of us is wrong. We have just had to learn our differences and how to work together as a team to get where we are going.

Just what are these differences, and how does that affect our being leaders?

BRAIN GAMES

Aside from the obvious physical differences between the sexes (indoor vs. outdoor plumbing), men's and women's brains are configured differently. For instance, women tend to have a larger prefrontal cortex (PFC) than men. The PFC is where our personality and social behavior skills develop. It is also where strategic planning takes place. The PFC is where all conditions, risks, and rewards are arranged to find the best way to proceed. Men tend to weigh these factors quickly and make fast and firm decisions, while women take longer to process all the available information before coming to a conclusion.

Joe and I have bought and sold many homes over the years. Although we've always ended up unified in the decision, our approach to the decision has been completely different. Our first home was a $52,000, 1500 square foot home built in 1880. When a local realtor knocked on our door saying she had a buyer who would pay whatever we wanted to have the home, Joe's answer was, "Sold!"

I, on the other hand, said, "I don't know. There's so much to think about. We'll have to get back to you." In my mind, it was my dream home. It didn't matter that we only had two bedrooms, and one bathroom, with only a tub and no shower (which was particularly uncomfortable for my 6'5" husband), and that our family was growing. Our young family had made memories there, and I had many more dreams to be fulfilled in my dream home. Besides the big front porch, fourteen-foot ceilings, and fireplaces in every room, I loved the quaint location and that it was walking distance to my best friend's house. I was concerned that even with a good offer on the sale that I'd never be able to replace this one-of-a-kind historic home.

"What do you mean you 'don't know'?" Joe asked. "It's an easy decision. Let's get the ball rolling tomorrow, before the buyer finds something else."

"Well," I said, "I really think we need to think this out more fully."

Joe was getting frustrated because I hesitated on a decision he thought was cut-and-dried. He didn't see that I was simply being who I was made to be—a woman. And women need to process through all of the details before they can come to a conclusion she will feel comfortable living with. I was not purposefully slowing things down. This was my way of leading so as not to overlook some critical detail. Men and women can clash if they refuse to acknowledge their differences, or they can happily work together if they each use their strengths and respect the strength of the other.

While women generally have a larger prefrontal cortex, they tend to have smaller amygdalae than men. The amygdala is sometimes called the "primitive brain," as this is where emotions such as fear, anger, and aggression reside. With this part of their brain smaller, women are often the calm, cool, and collected ones in leadership. Men, with more room in their amygdala to store up aggressive emotions, react more quickly and proactively to threats against themselves or their loved ones.

STRAIGHT TALK

Nothing shows the uniqueness of men and women as much as their way of talking. Even if a man and woman are basically saying the same thing, the way they say it can make it seem there is a wide gulf between them. Most men communicate to give or receive information; women use communication to build relationships. Men tend to be problem solvers; they want to cut through the chit-chat and get to a solution so they can move on. Some women want to talk out the problem so they can better understand how they are feeling about the situation, and then they will be able to move toward a solution.

Notice I said "some women" are like this. I am most assuredly not one of these "some women." I am typically very focused on a task or goal and want to use my "talk time" to accomplish what is before me. This will take some people aback at first. They don't expect "straight talk" coming from a very feminine woman. This is one of the reasons some see me as bossy. I'm not trying to put anyone down. I'm just trying to get things done in the right way and in a timely fashion so we can move on.

SOME WOMEN ARE NOT FACING A GLASS CEILING, BUT A FEELINGS CEILING.

FEELINGS CEILING

Another area where men and women leaders can differ is how they display emotions. Men tend to be stoic, holding their emotions at bay when they talk. Many women allow their emotions to drive the conversation, making others feel uncomfortable—especially if the emotional woman is their boss. You have heard the term "glass ceiling" used to describe how women don't get the same opportunities as men in business just because they are women. Sometimes that's true, although I'd like to explore another reason that can unseat women from tables of opportunity. I submit to you that we should take an honest look. Is it a really glass ceiling keeping women from rising as leaders? Sometimes instead of a glass ceiling, I see a "feelings ceiling." I work in a female empowering organization, yet I've seen women sabotage their opportunities by letting their emotions go on a rampage, breaking things and people along the way.

Over the years I've worked with great men who value women, who want women's perspectives, and who understand the benefit of having women in the room. I want more women and men in more rooms sharing ideas together. But as we team up, we have to realize there's a trade-off. We must check our emotions at the door—no crying at the table, sisters. Men need to check some of their behaviors at the door too—no locker-room talk, and please use your mixed company manners. Those who don't know how to approach leadership in a way that is relatable for both men and women are not going to have a seat at the table where decisions are made. I don't want the way I am as a woman to ever be the cause of not being at that table. I want my gender to be seen as a positive in working with and leading others.

There are those who cry out for equal rights for women when it seems what they really want are "special rights" as women. Some women feel they have been deprived of equality, and now it's payback time. The truth, however, is that no one wants emotional drama or complicated behavior from women (or men, for that matter). And it is sometimes emotionally-driven complicated behavior that keeps us from leadership positions.

Most men are not going to have problems with you as a leader—either alongside of them or over them—if you can just be who God has made you to be, not trying to get "special rights" because of your gender. I want you to be empowered to be your authentic self, the self who is a leader. This "authentic you" leader is going to be working with men and women, those younger than you and those older than you. You are going to need to learn how to merge who you are into the context of who God has placed on your team—those you are called to lead.

It took me so many years to really gain my leadership voice. I had people challenge me, saying, "You're a really strong leader. How come we don't see that in action in the church?" I always had this internal conflict going on: I felt I should be a sweet and smiling pastor's wife and keep my constructive opinions to myself, and yet I had wisdom for situations going on around me. I had to get to where I knew it was okay to lead with strength, just as God had wired me to do. I had to realize I could be like Deborah, a woman leader in a man's world.

This does not mean you should become someone you're not. This does not mean you need to adopt a male personality in order to lead. And it definitely doesn't mean rising in position at the expense of men. We are to work together as a team. We are each a piece of a great puzzle. Just as when you start linking jigsaw puzzle pieces together you begin to see the whole picture, so forming a team with the right players in the right spots allows you to see what God is doing. What's important to note here is that both women and men have important skill areas in which they naturally excel. Relying primarily on the strength of just one gender as leaders can result in an imbalance of perspectives and ideas. On the other hand, when women and men work side by side on the leadership team and in the boardroom, this diversity of perspectives can lead to more innovative thinking. This better balance, in turn, can result in greater productivity, improved engagement, higher profits, and a sustainable competitive advantage.

FIND YOUR PLACE

My family is football crazy. *All of us.* My husband, his dad, and all three of our boys played football. If I hadn't learned the ins and outs of the game, I would have felt left out. Believe me when I say I know football as well, if not better, than most men. And one of the first things I learned was that each player on the field has his own job to do. An offensive lineman can't do what the quarterback does. The nose guard can't do what the safety does. They all have their individual jobs to do, but when they each do what they are coached to do, they work together as a team. In football, teams, not individuals, win games.

Paul in his letter to the church at Corinth says the same thing about the Body of Christ as he compares it to the human body. "What if the foot complained that because it wasn't a hand, it didn't want to be in the body any longer? Or if the ear said because it wasn't beautiful like the eye, it didn't deserve to be a part of the body? And can you imagine what it would be like if the entire body were just one big eye?" (See 1 Corinthians chapter 12.) He goes on to say that God gives special honor to the lesser parts of the body, the parts that aren't seen but are vital to the health of the entire body. In other words, there is no unimportant limb or organ; they are all necessary if the body is to be healthy and function as it has been designed.

LEARN TO ACCEPT CRITICISM AND DEFLECT PRAISE.

The same thing we see in football and in the body is true in a church or in an organization. If everyone is doing the job they have been called to do, the organization functions smoothly and moves forward. But if even just a few people try to do what they are not called to do—if the running back tries to be the quarterback, or the liver acts like a stomach—trouble will ensue.

Each one of us is both a leader and a follower. We need to keep in our lanes. We need to lead those we are called to lead, and follow the person placed over us as a leader. Please don't get the idea I'm saying this is easy to do. It's not. It takes great humility as well as great confidence. You have to be willing both to speak up and to remain silent. Leaders must learn to accept criticism on themselves while deflecting praise to others. These are skills that take a lifetime to learn and perfect. It isn't easy—but what in life worth having is easy?

CHAPTER 9

HUMBLE UP

Jesus gathered them all together and said to them, "Those recognized as rulers of the people and those who are in top leadership positions rule oppressively over their subjects, but this is not the example you are to follow. You are to lead by a different model. If you want to be the greatest one, then live as one called to serve others. The path to promotion and prominence comes by having the heart of a bond-slave who serves everyone. For even the Son of Man did not come expecting to be served by everyone, but to serve everyone, and to give his life as the ransom price in exchange for the salvation of many."

Mark 10:42-45 (TPT)

"Serving others prepares you to lead others."

—Jim George

Preteen years weren't kind to me. I grew six inches one summer and I was already thin, so I looked anorexic going into the 7th grade. That, combined with a very bad haircut, (which could now be classified as a mullet), poor taste in clothes, a new set of braces, and skin problems brought on by hormone changes that also didn't help my emotional state. And did I mention that we moved to a new school district, where long-term friendships were already established, and it seemed no one was looking to invite me into their circle?

I was sitting at the cafeteria table by myself, hating life, when Sharon came over and invited me into her friend group. She was a sweet, humble girl, who said, "I used to sit by myself too, and then I made some friends. We'd love for you to be our friend." I am forever grateful to that girl. We honestly had nothing in common except for "friendlessness" and kindness. As time passed, we didn't share classes in our very large school, we didn't live in the same area or share hobbies. We each made different friends, yet we always happily greeted each other in the hallways when we'd run into each other. I couldn't look at her without overwhelming gratefulness that she took responsibility and did not allow me to stay in my state of loneliness. Very sadly, two years later, she took her own life. Upon receiving the news, I was in such a state of despair and guilt that I hadn't stayed closely in touch and that I had no idea of her pain that I had to call my parents to pick me up from school to process the grief.

It was during that time that my dad made me learn the only poem I've memorized to this day, "Outwitted" by Edwin Markham:

He drew a circle that shut me out —
Heretic, rebel, a thing to flout.
But Love and I had the wit to win:
We drew a circle that took him in!

My dad said, "Lori, if you're being left out, you just need to draw a circle that includes all of your excluders. You need to do what it says in Proverbs 18:24 (NKJV): *A man who has friends must himself be friendly....*" My dad lived by that model. So did Sharon. Humble leaders aren't about crushing other people on the way to the top.

They are about including others. Celebrating the success of others, and making a big deal of others. In fact, one of the core values at our church is "People are a Big Deal!"

Seems simple, but in a world where the first question is often, "How does this impact *me*?" and in a world where 93 million "selfies" are taken daily, humble leaders seem to be on the "endangered species" lists.

Don't let this shake you. We are not called to be "of this world." There is something greater waiting for us. Jesus has a different promotion plan than that of this culture.

OPPOSITE DAY

We all know them. You know, those who want to be the bride at every wedding and the corpse at every funeral. The trumpet players who are always tooting their own horns.

There are many women (and men) in leadership positions who are all style with no substance. They use industry buzzwords, name-drop those they met once, and pretend to be busy when actually they are putting up a façade, hoping no one sees through to the person they really are: ignorant and clueless about what it is they are supposed to be doing. Being naive and clueless is not a sin; as a matter of fact, those who admit they don't know how to do something show wisdom and are then able to learn and grow. It is those who wear a mask of perfection who are dangerous to themselves and to those they lead. I have seen all sorts of mask-wearing leaders in my life. Those who manipulate others so they can be promoted. Those with an entitlement attitude who refuse to be held accountable. Those who adopt the ways of our culture to get ahead. Those who think they are too big to receive constructive criticism. Those who are too busy to help others. Those who are not in touch with the struggles and cares of those they work with. This is so unlike Jesus. He came not seeking celebrity or a good reputation. He walked humbly with the sick, the lepers, the hungry; He came to be with the poor, the outcast. He came not to be served, but to serve. As we read in the Gospels, *"For even the Son of Man did not come expecting to be served by everyone, but to serve everyone, and to give his life in exchange for the salvation of many"* (Matthew 20:28 TPT). (See also Mark 10:45 and John 13:1-17.)

LEADERS AREN'T MADE IN GREENROOMS OR BOARDROOMS, BUT THE BEST LEADERS ARE IN TOUCH WITH REAL PEOPLE.

Leaders aren't made in greenrooms or boardrooms; the best leaders are in touch with real people. We've had the privilege of hosting Dr. Gary Chapman, author of *The Five Love Languages*, at our church a few times. He has sold multiple millions of books, and yet he told us that he still takes counseling appointments at his local church. When we asked him why, he said, "I've got to stay in touch with the pain of people." Success can make you a talking head with no heart. Just look at our politicians and celebrities, who often become echo chambers of a world that can only be enjoyed by a few. God forbid that the culture of narcissism finds a home in the lives of us as believers.

Every day of leadership is "opposite day" when you're leading like Jesus. His last act of leadership before His death wasn't picking up a title but picking up a towel and washing the feet of His disciples, even knowing that some would betray or deny Him.

Sister, being a leader is a great responsibility. Whether you are a leader of one—yourself—or tens of thousands, you must lead with respect, integrity, and humility.

It is this last trait—humility—that is so often misunderstood and mischaracterized. And yet without a true understanding of humility—and putting it to practice in our lives—we cannot truly walk with the Lord, let alone be the leader He has called us to be. Just what does true humility look like? Before we answer that, let's see what humility does not look like.

WHAT HUMILITY IS NOT

C. S. Lewis said, "Humility is not thinking less of yourself; it's thinking of yourself less." The great South African preacher Andrew Murray said almost the same thing: "The humble person is not one who thinks meanly of himself; he simply does not think of himself at all."

Humility does not mean you hate who you are or what you look like, and it certainly doesn't mean believing you are worthless. Humility means recognizing other people's worth and talents, while also recognizing your own gifts and worth.

Humility shouldn't be confused with low self-esteem, fearfulness, or feelings of inferiority. And while being humble requires admitting our own difficulties, shortcomings, and weaknesses, it doesn't mean we should make a show of them. Humility means living in the truth, accepting that we aren't perfect. Humility isn't about putting ourselves down, but about realism. Many people think they're humble when in reality they're always talking about how unfortunate and lowly they are. This causes them to focus entirely on themselves, which is a form of pride.

True humility doesn't mean continually comparing ourselves to others. Doing this isn't humility; it is turning inward and only seeing others as a threat. When you are humble, you don't need to feel that you're better than others. At the same time, humble people don't consistently yield to what other people want them to do, nor let themselves be manipulated. They simply see their own place without having to debate who's better or worse off. Humility is recognizing the truth about yourself and being at peace with it.

Humility does not mean you must be a doormat. You can be a leader and be humble; in fact, humility is an excellent trait in a leader. It means that you voice your opinion when someone asks for it. It means asking questions, admitting failures, and seeking help when you don't know how to do something. A humble leader acts boldly and decisively to help those under her care, even if it means going against the flow.

The best example of a humble but uncompromising and bold leader I know of is my husband. One of the things that attracted me to Joe was that I'd never seen someone who could so confidently own a room, yet make every single person feel like they are the most important person in the room. He is the most agenda-free person I know. Because he has such a dynamic personality, along with being full of wisdom and humor, he's always asked to the "head table" of any event. Yet, he's almost always the last person to leave the building, and it's usually because he's making conversation with the events team, the ones staying late to clean up. He's not just thanking them for their service, he is asking them their life stories and their future dreams. He wouldn't be called "strategic" in his relationships. He isn't trying to get to the top of any food chains, yet any ambitious person would envy the leaders he has in his phone contacts, leaders who call him for advice and friendship.

TRUE HUMILITY

The early Church fathers called humility the "mother of all virtues." From humility, they said, flows all other virtues we are to walk in. What virtues were they speaking of? From the earliest days of Christianity, there have been three "theological" and four "cardinal" virtues. The first three—the theological—virtues are found at the end of the great love chapter in 1 Corinthians 13: *faith, hope,* and *love.* The next four date back to the Greek philosopher Plato. They are *wisdom, courage, self-control,* and *justice.* God wants us to possess each of these virtues, have them constantly increase, and live according to them. Yet we can only forge these virtues in our lives when we humbly recognize and accept the areas where we are weak and need to grow. We will never stand tall with God unless we first lay ourselves down before Him. In James we read, *Humble yourselves in the sight of the Lord, and He will lift you up* (James 4:10 NKJV).

Just what is humility? And how do we get it?

Psychologists use the term "authenticity" more than humility, yet it leads to the same end. Authenticity is living the truth about yourself, being honest with you and others. This is the baseline of humility—honestly admitting to yourself just who you are, the good and the bad. Humility is a sign of psychological and spiritual maturity; it leads to freedom. Rather than a series of behavioral "rules," we must try to live up to, humility is a way of being and of relating to others honestly. It is seen by the way you accept and value *you*.

We already saw that humility is not putting ourselves down and thinking we are "no good at anything." That isn't humility—it's pride. Pride shines the light on us, while humility is about focusing our lives on God and not on ourselves. It means accepting that we aren't the center of the universe, and that the world doesn't revolve around us. Humility leads to self-knowledge that makes us more human and more aware of our weakness and limitations, without pretending to be something we aren't. This is an excellent thing, for Paul writes, *Therefore I will boast all the more gladly of my weaknesses, so that the power of Christ may rest upon me* (2 Corinthians 12:9).

Are you starting to see how humility is key to being the leader God has called you to be?

Humble leaders want to improve themselves, and can do so because they live in reality and the truth. They aren't proud, because they recognize their defects willingly; they aren't negative about themselves, because they believe they can change in response to

God's call to holiness and with the help of His grace. Being courageous enough to see and acknowledge our mistakes makes us capable of growing and maturing.

At the same time, genuinely humble leaders rejoice in the good of other people and in the greatness that surrounds them. They are free from inferiority complexes and from the need to compare themselves to others. Humble people are free from a constant need for praise, recognition, or affirmation for their virtues because they know who they are and that they have worth as they are.

IF YOU AREN'T TEACHABLE, YOU AREN'T TEAMABLE.

When it comes to leading my staff, I have a saying, "If you aren't *teachable*, you aren't *teamable*." We never arrive. We never stop growing. In our church, every event has a debrief and there's always something to learn to make the next event even better. Another saying around our organization (not original to us) is, "Notetakers are history-makers." There's nothing worse to me, as a leader, than preparing for a meeting where I'm investing in and developing a person, only to have him/her show up without taking notes. They're saying to me, "I already know everything you're going to say," or "I don't need to grow." And there are those who take notes but never again look at them or make adjustments. They are lacking the trait of humility that must be present in order to grow as a leader and as a person.

True humility, therefore, is a source of confidence, courage, and freedom. Humble leaders don't go begging for recognition and don't get discouraged when they don't get it, because their contentment doesn't depend on another person's opinion. By contrast, those who are proud are very sensitive to criticism and are easily wounded and discouraged.

It's said that the three hardest things to say are 1) I need help, 2) I'm sorry, and 3) Worcestershire sauce. I'm not sure about that last one, but the first two can only be spoken by someone with a truly humble spirit.

Being genuinely humble and living authentically makes other people feel comfortable. They're easy to be around because they don't feel the need to impose their opinion or to be right all the time. They aren't afraid of criticism because they don't need to protect a false image of themselves. Humble leaders know how to recognize when they are wrong, ask forgiveness, look for help, and publicly acknowledge their own mistakes. They are grateful, able to recognize other people's generosity, and are empathetic, knowing how to be compassionate with other people's shortcomings.

In short, unlike pride that creates negative, unproductive people who never realize their potential, true humility makes us more human, free, mature, compassionate, and grateful, able to lead others in strength and confidence.

Finally, a humble leader knows that everything she has is from God. Everything. Not just her material goods, but her very soul. Her very life. She makes Galatians 6:14 one of her life verses.

But God forbid that I should boast except in the cross of our Lord Jesus Christ, by whom the world has been crucified to me, and I to the world (NKJV).

HUMBLE LEADERS IN ACTION

Jon Bloom of Desiring God Ministries says, "Not thinking much of themselves means that humble people prefer windows to mirrors. Desiring to see the glory of God in everything frees them from needing to see how everything else reflects on them. Humble people view other people as God's marvelous image-bearers, windows to God's glory, not as mirrors that enhance or diminish their own self-image. But this also means they aren't absorbed by how others view them. They aren't worried about reading the 'right' books, seeing the 'right' movies, listening to the 'right' music, living in the 'right' home, having the 'right' job, being seen with the 'right' people, etc. That's a mirror mind-set. They view these things as windows to see and savor God's glory."

From this, we see that humble leaders don't worry about what others think of them—they are free to make decisions and carry out strategies they know are going to be profitable, even if they aren't understood or appreciated at the time. I've heard it said this way: "Your opinion of me is not my problem." Too harsh? Read on, my sister.

Bloom also says that truly humble leaders can sometimes come across as harsh and offensive. "Humble people," says Bloom, "being without guile, say it like it is. And saying it like it is can sting, and even sound condemning. But there is a qualitative difference between the offensiveness of the proud and the offensiveness of the humble. The proud offend to exalt or defend themselves and control or manipulate others. The humble offend in order to advance the truth for the glory of God and ultimate good of others. Humble offensiveness may not be popular, but it's always loving."

We see this "humble offensiveness" in Scripture. Jesus did not hesitate to say it like it is, calling out His disciples for their lack of faith on numerous occasions. He referred to the religious leaders as wicked hypocrites and whitewashed tombs. Paul called the Galatians "foolish" because they wanted to return to the law instead of living by grace through faith. Humble leaders are not afraid to speak the truth—lay it on the line—as long as it is said in love.

I believe we live in the most sensitive time in history. People get their feelings hurt, or are, as they call it, "triggered" so easily that it's difficult to have conversations that would be beneficial for growth. As a leader, I've felt the inner conflict when I know exactly what needs to be said to bring an adjustment to someone, yet not knowing if it will send them into an emotional spiral, thus stifling their potential to progress. As a leader, I'm left thinking, "If only they could grow in this area, then they'd be more respected, or promotable, or credible as a leader." But I can't share that with them because they are not humble enough to receive it.

If you look at these "humble offensiveness" examples in the Bible through the lens of today's hyper "feelings-ness" generation, you may think Jesus or Paul were rude, but as someone who has grown through these types of conversations in my own life, I'm forever grateful for hard conversations. Let's not confuse hard conversations with harsh conversations. Proverbs 25:11 says it well: *A word fitly spoken is like apples of gold in a setting of silver.*

"I have good news and bad news. You have cancer, but the batting average is good on this kind." Those are the words I heard upon waking from anesthesia after a biopsy on April 16, 1992, (while eight months pregnant). Nothing in me said, "That ruined my day" or "That really hurt my feelings." The truth isn't always what we want to hear, but it is what we need to hear to heal or to improve. My doctor's words were a communication clinic for sharing the truth the right way—straight-forward, compassionate, and hope filled. After a month of testing me for everything known to man, the words, "You have cancer," were a relief. It thrust me into a new season—instead of continuing to ask questions, we could now focus on solutions.

Let's not make this more complicated than we need to. Learning to be a humble leader is acting with the best interests of others in your sight at all times. My doctor, no question, had my best interest in mind when he gave me those results. Do you have the listeners' best interest in mind when you're confronting them, or do you want them to despair by your correction? Do you need to get something off your chest, no matter how it affects them? Venting is not healthy for the one receiving the blast of anger, nor is it healthy for the one doing the blasting. Those humble in heart will find that their anger is quickly channeled into healthy and helpful words and expressions.

Truly humble leaders simply spend more time thinking about others than about themselves. Philippians 2:3-4 is a daily challenge for the humble leader.

Do nothing from selfish ambition or conceit, but in humility count others more significant than yourselves. Let each of you look not only to his own interests, but also to the interests of others.

Or, as we read it in *The Message,*

Don't push your way to the front; don't sweet-talk your way to the top. Put yourself aside, and help others get ahead. Don't be obsessed with getting your own advantage. Forget yourselves long enough to lend a helping hand.

Humility in action in a family, a church, or a business gathers people together into one united group, all working toward the same goals, all feeling valued for their contributions. But this must start with the leader. As you consistently display humility in what you say and what you do, others will be drawn to the silent strength that is inherent in humility. David Guzik of Enduring Word Media writes, "As we esteem others better, we will naturally have a concern for their needs and concerns; this sort of outward-looking mentality naturally leads to unity among the people of God. If I am considering you above me, and you are considering me above you, a marvelous thing happens: we have a community where everyone is looked up to, and no one is looked down on."

STRONG LEADERS HAVE THE STRENGTH OF HUMILITY.

To be a strong leader, you must first learn the strength of humility. So, my sister, Humble Up!

CHAPTER 10

PURPOSE UP

Whatever you do, work at it with all your heart,
as working for the Lord, not for human masters.

Colossians 3:23 (NIV)

"God has created me to do Him some definite service;
He has committed some work to me which He has not
committed to another. I have my mission—I may never
know it in this life, but I shall be told it in the next."

—John Henry Newman

If you were to ask me to describe my typical day, I would answer that there is no "typical day" in the Champion household. Every day we are presented with a new path to explore, a new battle to fight, a new mountain to climb. But I can share some of the things I find myself doing often, whether that be hourly, daily, or weekly. I'm always answering emails. I get one knocked out, and in the amount of time it takes to do that, five more have populated my inbox, waiting for a response. Decisions beckon my attention—whether it's strategic ones, financial ones, or "what's for dinner?" ones. I remember the day I got a Blackberry phone. I had my very first email by 5 a.m. from one of my co-workers with a list of situations to deal with. My life changed that day. Gone were the days of going into the office for work. The work now comes to me, while still in my pajamas, long before 9 a.m., and way past 5 p.m., any day of the week, no matter where I am in the world.

Some days, I'm writing a message for a conference. Some days, I'm meeting with staff or talking about launching a new Celebration campus or adding a ministry or leading a team meeting. Many days I'm traveling, as Joe and I serve on many boards, give oversight to several ministry leaders, and have overseas campuses. I still have unending laundry to wash, bills to pay, groceries to buy, holidays to plan, and dinner to cook. Cooking is my job, not because I'm the woman of the family (some of my female friends don't lift a finger in the kitchen thanks to their chef-level husbands!). It's because if my husband cooked, we'd have popcorn every night. He had one last semester to finish at school after playing college football where he didn't have an athletic department meal plan, so that's all he ate: popcorn. He also admits he never once changed the sheets during those four months, and he doesn't take on that responsibility in our home either.

"BEEING" BUSY

As you can tell, most days I'm busy as a bee. But does that mean I'm being productive or living according to the purpose to which I've been called? Deborah, as a judge in Israel, must have had similar demands on her time; she must have had many duties to perform, cases to hear, and decisions to render. Deborah—whose name means "bee"—was not "busy as a bee." We don't see her rushed or stressed out, even in the face of oppression from an enemy. When Barak tells Deborah, "I'll lead men into battle as the Lord called me to do, but only if you will go with me," we don't hear Deborah respond, "Oh, I would if I could. But you ought to see my in-basket. My calendar is full for the next six months. But I'll let you know if a cancelation comes up." Deborah was able to go immediately with Barak for one reason: She was laser-focused on doing the will of the Lord.

You know the saying, "If you want to get something done, give it to a busy person." I was with a friend of mine recently who is one of those people. She's a corporate leader, a church leader, a fitness enthusiast, an Energizer bunny, and she has just become an apiarist, or beekeeper. I was conversing with her about my book, and mentioned the meaning of the name Deborah. Turns out you can learn a lot about leadership from bees and the extraordinary beehive system.

Bees get a bad rap for appearing so busy all of the time, but all of their efforts are focused on one thing: feeding the queen and her brood, those baby bees who will soon grow and take the place of the ones who are today doing the work of the hive, thus insuring the survival of the hive. They are not engaged in "busy work" to look important. All of the workers—and they are all females—stay focused on the needs of the hive. None have aspirations of one day becoming queen. There is no time for jealousy, greed, or pride. There are a lot of mouths to feed to keep the hive alive.

It's true that there is only one queen bee in a hive. But guess what? The queen doesn't live a life of luxury, and she is not irreplaceable. The queen bee was born to carry out two jobs: to lay eggs (up to 2,000 a day), and to give direction through pheromones (scents) so the bees know what their assignments are that day. I said she is not irreplaceable, and she isn't. When she begins to lay fewer eggs than necessary to keep the hive going, the workers will choose a larva to become the new queen, feeding it special food called "royal jelly." When the new queen emerges and mates, the old queen is then attacked and killed by workers in the hive. That's what happens to leaders in our world as well. When things are going great, the leader is held in high esteem;

but as soon as there is a downward trend or profits not what they once were or growth is no longer taking place, the "worker bees" in the organization (be it a nonprofit foundation, a business, or a church) decide it is time for a new leader. We have all known of instances where the founder of an organization begins to coast, no longer seeking to fulfill their purpose. You know the kind—someone who "retires" without leaving. Often this person is forced out of what she started, and the organization goes in a whole new direction.

Bees—whether the queen, workers (who are all female), or drones (males)—have a singular purpose: to keep the hive alive. Each knows its role in doing so. Workers, the females, are responsible for foraging for food, feeding the young, cleaning the hive, keeping it warm in the winter and cool in the summer, and guarding the hive against intruders. Male bees—the drones—live for only one thing: to mate with the queen. (Does this sound familiar?) After they mate, they die. That's it. Mate, then die. The female bees literally do everything to keep the hive going, including replacing the queen when necessary.

We can only take this bee illustration so far. I mean, we don't really want our husbands to die after mating, do we? And while women want and need to be empowered, we don't want to be overpowered by having every task and duty assigned to us. A female bee's lifecycle is from four to six weeks long, no doubt owing to the fact that they have so much to do. This is not the way I am suggesting you live your life. We are all prone to burnout. A good definition of burnout is "work without purpose." Bees work long and hard, but their work is purposeful; and when they die, they have given their all for others. There is a lot we can learn from bees about purposeful leadership and purposeful living.

LET PURPOSE DRIVE ACTIVITIES

There is a story of a woman whose first job was as a dishwasher in a hospital. She could have thought of her job as invaluable, mundane.

But her boss modeled leading on purpose by telling her, "Your job is not just washing dishes. You are part of the healing process here by providing patients with a clean and healthy environment where they can heal quickly and go home to their families." The woman no longer looked at herself as "merely" a dishwasher. She saw herself as part of a team of healers. She saw purpose in every plate and spoon she scrubbed and did her job with passion.

Wouldn't you be more passionate about washing dishes if that was your purpose? Purpose can be found even in the most ordinary duties, when we have the right perspective.

King David, the ruler of a nation, said,

I would rather be a doorkeeper in the house of my God
  than dwell in the tents of wickedness.

Psalm 84:10

There's purpose in door-keeping in God's house. The doorkeeper is the first person to welcome someone into an environment where God can change a person's life. Once in the presence of God, someone can experience restoration in their marriage, realization of their purpose, or their broken heart can be mended, like mine was a few decades ago, when a shell of a young woman walked into a new church filled with hopelessness after her father's untimely death. Had I encountered a doorkeeper with a bad attitude, maybe my life would be different today.

We have a man named Steve who is the first person to arrive at our church every single service. He's done this for ten or more years. He leads the team that sets out directional signs on the road leading to our property, and then he and the team cheerfully welcome people to church. It doesn't matter what the weather is, he serves with a smile on his face. Thousands have been saved in our church, and it's not just because of the great preaching; it's because of people like

Steve. It's because he has a purpose way bigger than what may look like a mundane volunteer job.

Before each of our services, our volunteers (we call them our "Dream Team") have a high-energy rally. It opens with a worship song, then someone shares a testimony or two of how lives have been changed in a recent service, and they are inspired to remember the "why" behind what they each do in their dream team roles—every person on that team has a meaningful purpose to fulfill our first core value—that people experience Christ in our worship gathering. Without a compelling purpose—both for us as leaders and for those we lead—all our efforts are just putting in time. Our minds might be engaged, but our hearts are not. When you get your team inspired about a purpose, their hearts will follow.

BETTER TOGETHER

There can be thousands of bees in a single hive who need to work together in order to survive. Survival is a strong motivator. But we don't want to just survive, we want to thrive. For your business, ministry, or family to thrive, your team/family must work together toward a common goal. Bees have no challenges with their ego nor hidden agendas they have to deal with. Instead, each bee is focused only on obtaining the goals for the betterment of the entire colony, not just for themselves.

For your team to really understand what *life together* means, you as the leader must lay aside your ego and work for the betterment of all involved—your customers (or congregation), your employees and volunteers, and—if you have any—for your investors. Transparency is key in gaining the cooperation of others working for and with you. If your business is experiencing challenges, sit down with your team for a brainstorming session—and listen to their ideas. Be prepared for some "ouch" moments. I opened up a discussion about an overloaded events calendar at work recently, and the team brought up cutting something that I personally love. After assessing the wins of the event, we chose to keep it (phew!). What pleased me was that our team felt it was safe to bring it up in the first place. In a healthy organization, it's important to protect your core values, but how you accomplish those values can become "sacred cows" that become ineffective or outdated over time.

We have led our home in the same way. There's no question about who the parents are—we aren't afraid to parent. At the same time, we are not dictators. We have never shied away from open, but honoring, discussions with our children. We took our kids with us to a church conference many years ago, and my oldest son, Mason, went with me to a breakout session where a very well-known pastor was speaking about leadership. He was asked about work-life balance, and he said, "The reason my family is successful is because my wife gave up her very successful career to stay at home, and to provide a haven for me when I come home from the office. We don't really talk about church at home. Our kids have a mother completely devoted to them and not distracted by career or other things." In all honesty, I felt like a failure as a parent, and as my son was sitting there listening to the same thing, I thought, "I'm sure he feels completely cheated." Instead of being defensive of how I have worked full time for most of his life and not always provided a "haven-type atmosphere," I said, "Mason, you can be honest with me. Do you feel like I've given too much time to work and that you would have rather had a mom like that pastor's wife?" Inside I braced myself for what my brutally honest, sometimes harsh firstborn would say. He said, "I'm so glad you are the way you are. I want my wife to be strong like you are and to work with me."

I hope you aren't hearing that I'm being critical of how that pastor's family does life and how his wife gave up her career and stayed home. I believe they did exactly what God called them to do. I know it took sacrifice on so many levels, and I admire the commitment of every stay-at-home mom. The point is, keep an open dialogue in family and in career. We are talking about living, changing organisms (made up of people, not robots), and we have to listen and adjust our approach as different seasons evolve. You can't have it all and be it all, all at the same time.

As important as it is to transparently communicate, it's equally important that you celebrate. Did you just accomplish a big goal? Share that with the team, in both a congratulatory announcement and celebration, whether it's bringing in lunch, giving "shout-outs" during staff meetings, or handing out bonuses. October 1, 2001, we celebrated our first year of Celebration Church with our original launch team—Joe, me, and our three boys, ages nine, five, and twenty months. To celebrate, we went to Chuck E. Cheese! I remember thinking over a year that we barely survived, looking at those little boys thinking about how much they sacrificed—parents with out-of-control schedules and an out-of-balance home life where they were plopped in front of the TV way too often while we finished working at our home office. They didn't sign up for it, but God graced them for it, because He placed them in our family, a family He called to be church planters. We still value celebrating with our original team—although now we get to celebrate with grown-ups. We value having a fun atmosphere. Work hard. Play hard.

Be purposeful in building a team atmosphere. Don't hide in your office with a "do not disturb" sign on the door. Be out where your team is. Don't run from challenges. Bring your team together to identify ways you as the leader and your business or ministry must change to vault over the challenge. The same principles apply to your home. Be present. Be intentional. Be on purpose. Be unified. Your family is the greatest team you'll ever get to lead.

COMMUNICATION IS KEY

Communication is vital in a beehive. To feed the incredible amount of larva that hatch every day, a large amount of food—pollen and nectar—must be gathered and brought to the hive. Bees are always on the lookout for fresh sources of these nutrients. When a bee finds a patch of flowers just dripping with nectar and pollen, she doesn't keep this information to herself. Instead, she hurries back to the hive and dances. And the way she struts and grooves gives precise directions to the other foraging bees to find the all-you-can-eat buffet (or, should I say, *bee-fet*). Just as bees best communicate in dance, your business must have a solid communication structure in place. Team members must be confident and comfortable enough to raise the red flag if needed, ask their colleagues for help, or reach out to you for guidance. If bees were unable to effectively communicate with one another, their very survival would be at stake.

COMMUNICATION IS THE FOOD OF LEADERSHIP.

Communication is the food of leadership. It has been said, "People are down on what they are not up on." Think about that for a second. Where there is a void of communication, sometimes the gaps are filled with negative thoughts, which produce negative momentum. Communication is critical to your organization's survival. You must be clear in your communication to those who work with and for you. Don't be vague in what you want done; be specific. Be clear and concise in your expectations and goals. Model good communication not only in your words, but also in your mannerisms, your emotions, your presence. Just being where the work is done speaks volumes to your team.

Spend time weekly talking with your team, individually and as a group. It doesn't have to take a lot of time. That way, you will have time to listen to challenges and complaints, recommend solutions, and then move on. After all, once the bee has finished her dance, she doesn't wait around for applause. She gets back to work.

LEARN TO ADAPT

Bees don't gather exclusively in the most productive flower patches, and for good reason. When a lucrative vein of nectar is discovered, the entire colony doesn't rush off to mine it no matter how enriching the short-term benefits. The colony has internalized a very important natural rule: someday the nectar in that location will stop flowing and they need to be prepared to rapidly reallocate resources to other productive sites. As the bees clearly advise through their behavior, overexploiting a rich patch just because it is there is a death trap. A hive's survival depends on their ability to adapt. If environmental factors such as extreme temperatures or drought threaten their survivability, bees will relocate the entire hive to a better location. They don't let personal feelings or the notion of "we've always done it this way" interfere with their survivability.

When the colony knows it must move, it puts the plan into action right away. Scout bees are sent out to look for options; when they return, they dance to show the direction and just how good they think the new location can be. Then more scout bees go to see if the first scouts were accurate in their description; in other words, they do their due diligence. Once a spot is settled on, the entire hive moves and settles in quickly. Changing circumstances means change for everyone.

As a leader, show how you can adapt quickly to change, embracing "different" without longing for the good ol' days—which really, when you think about it, weren't all that good. The same is true in our own lives. God calls us to walk with Him, which indicates He is moving forward, not backward, and not standing still.

LET OTHERS LEAD

Yes, there is a queen bee, but she isn't a tyrannical leader laying down laws. Rather, she is a servant to her hive, laying eggs and producing more quality bees to help ensure the hive continues. The queen knows her role within the colony and performs her duties while trusting the hive to do their duties. With many thousands of employed workers, the queen couldn't possibly direct all of the actions in the field from her place in the hive. While the queen is the heart and soul of the hive, she is by no means the only leader. Those closest to the information make the relevant decisions.

Decentralization is one of the hallmarks of the honeybee colony. Foraging decisions, for example, are made by the foragers. The information doesn't travel up to the queen and back again. If you are thinking of shifting greater power away from the organizational core and into the field, however, consider these facts first:

- bees have clear objectives;

- they are excellent communicators and are able to quickly take in and consolidate information—and transform that information into coordinated action; and

- they are reliable workers that are very good at what they do.

Deborah modeled this by giving Barak clear objectives—she told him how many soldiers to gather and where to get them from. She knew Barak was a good communicator—he went forth to gather soldiers and was able to convince 10,000 to follow him into battle. And Deborah trusted Barak to do what he was tasked to do—defeat the enemy army.

"BEE" A SERVANT

As much as we are leaders in our church, ministry, or business, guiding others to achieve our vision for the company, we are also servants to our team. For me, that meant stepping into gaps when we've had them. I have a degree in journalism/advertising. There was a time when I did everything related to communications—designing ads for the newspaper, writing press releases and announcements, editing informational pamphlets, entering content for the website ... all of it. As the church has grown, we have a whole team to do that, and now my leadership is more at the 30,000 feet level—visionary and strategic. As much as I love to write, I'm not writing content for the worship guide handouts anymore. However, we were recently in need of a staff writer, and I found myself to be the best person for the job until the role was filled. The biggest takeaway from my involvement was not me showing them that I'm a competent announcement-writer but that I'm a "whatever it takes" leader.

Several years ago, my husband was speaking at the Hillsong Men's Conference. I accompanied him and was spending the day with Bobbie Houston, who has the biggest women's conference in the world, with events on multiple continents. While there, proofs for her conference magazine came in, and she went over every single word, telling one of her global women's leaders (who needed to translate it) her intention behind every word choice. With a team of hundreds, if not thousands, this leader wasn't too big to get involved in the details especially when it came to the language of her event.

I have another friend who leads a huge church—along with her husband—in Florida. They recently needed an overhaul in their Next Generations department, and she stepped in, restored it to health and identified the leaders who would take the team into the next season. Great leaders know when it's time to not just be out in front, but to get in the trenches.

Other times, I'm the one who needs to step out of the way of my team. My team knows what they're doing, and they don't need (or want!) me micromanaging details, so I need to get out of their way and let them do what they do best. You show great leadership aptitude when those who work for you are happy and fulfilled in what they are doing. The traditional "my way or the highway" style of leadership has been replaced by new management practices based on collaboration and trust. The new practice is to not just tell employees what to do, but why they are doing it and how it fits within the company's larger structure. By creating a company culture with a clear purpose and defined values, your employees will feel they are connected to something larger and that they have a voice that is being heard. Such practices will help increase their productivity and engagement. The hive survives only if all of the bees—from the queen to the bee whose job it is to clean up the trash—know they are all working together in the same direction for the same goal.

Purpose will never be contained in a job description. Your purpose is not your title. Allow me to share this story to show you what I mean.

YOUR PURPOSE IS NOT YOUR TITLE.

Our CFO is a brilliant woman who has taken our organization to many "next levels" through her extensive education and experience. We have a board of directors with profound knowledge and experience in their individual industries—some lead multi-billion-dollar companies, a couple are attorneys, CEO's, and a world-renowned doctor. She is impressive even to them, and they are at boardroom tables where financial statements have many more zeroes. Sometimes in ministry, you don't see the behind the scenes of what fuels our growth. You won't see this woman on stage, preaching a message, but she is just as in purpose as those who invite people to an altar to receive Christ.

In the last couple years, she's had a "come to purpose" moment. She asked to meet me for lunch, and her opening words were, "I've dreaded this conversation for the entire time I've worked here, close to ten years. If you want me to resign after this meeting, I completely understand. My husband and closest circle of friends who have ministered to me have been fasting and praying for this meeting." My imagination began to run wild. As a ministry leader, I've heard so many shocking things that I can barely be shocked, and she of all people would know that, as she has worked alongside us in an "it's okay to not be okay" environment for a long time.

Some of her past, before-Christ decisions had loomed over her, causing so much shame that she believed the lie that everyone but she could be forgiven. She meticulously, like the CPA she is, set forth the facts, and at the end, I said, "Is that all?" she nodded yes. "What took you so long to tell me? The enemy has been trying to keep you in bondage to the very pain that is meant to be your purpose." If you are looking for purpose, you can usually trace it back to your pain. I said, "You are a trophy to the grace of God, and God wants you to use your story to see more people set free by the very same amazing grace. So now, in addition to overseeing the stewardship of our ministry, she has started a ministry for women living in the same shame that isolated and imprisoned her for so many years. There were so many people on the other side of her coming clean about her past, her pain, and her saying "yes" to purpose. Her purpose has empowered others to walk in purpose.

Deborah, as a judge in Israel, is a model of a strong leader in what she did and what she empowered others to do. In our next chapter, we are going to see what one of these empowered people did.

CHAPTER 11

BUCKLE UP

If you wait for perfect conditions,
you will never get anything done.

Ecclesiastes 11:4 (TLB)

"Most of us go through life as failures, because we are waiting
for the 'time to be right' to start doing something worthwhile.
Do not wait. The time will never be 'just right.' Start where you
stand, and work with whatever tools you may have at your
command, and better tools will be found as you go along."

—Napoleon Hill

Let's return to the story of Deborah as found in the book of Judges. She was a judge in Israel, one who men and women sought for counsel. We also read that Deborah was a prophetess, one who could speak forth what the Spirit of God put in her heart. It was in both of these roles that Deborah called Barak and told him that the Lord wanted him to raise an army to go into battle against Israel's enemy. Barak was willing to obey as long as Deborah would go with him.

"I will go with you," she said, "but this venture will bring you no glory, because the Lord will leave Sisera to fall into the hands of a woman."

You might be thinking, and Barak probably did, that Deborah meant herself. As we have seen, the name "Deborah" means "honeybee," so Barak may have thought that this "bee" was going to sting Sisera and free the Jews from their oppressors. But Deborah didn't mean she was the woman who would do this. Then just who was the woman who would deal with Sisera? It was Jael, whose name means "mountain goat." Jael was the wife of Heber, a Kenite and a metalworker. We read about Heber in Judges chapter four.

Now Heber the Kenite had separated from the Kenites, the descendants of Hobab the father-in-law of Moses, and had pitched his tent as far away as the oak in Zaanannim, which is near Kedesh (Judges 4:11).

Heber was a descendent of Moses' father-in-law, and thus a friend of the Israelites. He was also on friendly terms with Jabin, and pitched his tent about halfway between Israel and Jabin's kingdom in Canaan. He had "separated" from his ancestral tribe, Kenites. Many translations make this seem to be a natural thing for Heber to do. Maybe he moved away from his relatives to have more space. But the Hebrew word used here for separate, *"padar,"* means to be scattered or alienated, perhaps by force. In other words, Heber had a past, something that caused him to lose the good graces of his family. He could have moved to avoid accusations or interrogations of what he had done. And if Heber was tainted by what he had done, this stain was attached to his wife. Yet Jael overcame this past to be used by God at just the right time.

Barak's army routed the Canaanite army, making Sisera run for his life. Sisera came to the village of Heber and Jael, with Barak hot on his trail. Jael spotted Sisera and waved him toward her tent.

"Come into my tent, my lord," said Jael. "Don't be afraid—come on in." So Sisera entered her tent, exhausted and extremely afraid.

"I'm thirsty," said Sisera. "Please give me some water." Instead, Jael gave him some milk—a treat for sure, but with a characteristic Jael was well aware of: Milk can make someone very sleepy. On top of Sisera's exhaustion from battle and from running as fast as he could to escape Barak, the milk no doubt cast him into an even deeper sleep. Jael, just like her namesake—the mountain goat—was very nimble on her feet and a fast thinker. When Sisera fell asleep, Jael found the tools she was skilled in using—a hammer and tent pegs. These were tools Jael had handled often when putting up tents. In that nomadic culture, the men would take care of gathering and herding livestock to the next location while the women would oversee the packing of household goods and taking down the tents. When they arrived at the next spot, the women—in this case, Jael—would erect the tents, stretch the cords, and drive in the pegs with hammers to keep the tent secure in the face of the desert winds. This was considered "women's work" at that time. I doubt Jael ever thought that her skill at driving tent pegs would allow her to gain a great victory for Israel. Yet here she was, faced with a once-in-a-lifetime opportunity to kill a great enemy of God's people. God never wastes an experience that leads to learning a skill.

You may think the experiences you have had—learning how to get stains out of clothes, how to enter data into a computer, how to operate office machines—are too commonplace and simplistic to offer for God's use. We tend to think only those with a public platform, like preachers, teachers, or writers, can be used for God's purposes. But He can and will use all that we do if we will make ourselves available to Him, and will rise for the occasion He places before us.

Jael was accomplished with a hammer and tent pegs. She picked these up, crept up to the sleeping Sisera, and nailed his head to the floor—literally. When Barak arrived in the village, Jael went out to meet him.

"Come here," she said, "and I'll show you the man you're looking for." Barak went into her tent and found the general of the army who had oppressed Israel for generations dead, a tent peg driven through his temple. This set in motion events that led to Israel being completely freed from their oppressors. In the last verses of Judges 4 we read, *So on that day Israel saw God defeat Jabin, the Canaanite king. And from that time on Israel became stronger and stronger against King Jabin until they finally destroyed him* (Judges 4:23-24 NLT).

Jael was a woman with a past—her husband's mysterious separation from his tribe—and only one skill we know of, using a hammer to drive in tent pegs. Yet because of her willingness to be used by God in a bold way, a great enemy of the people of God was destroyed.

YOUR TOOL BELT

Just as Jael didn't know that Sisera would be coming near her tent on the day she killed him, we never know when the Lord will bring an opportunity to work with and for Him. Thus, it's essential as a Christian leader to always have your tool belt buckled and ready. What are the tools we should each carry with us? I have five tools I believe you and I must have on our tool belts in order to be effective leaders.

1. Church

While on this earth, Jesus worked to establish His Church through His disciples. This was not an afterthought; it was a priority of our Lord to create a tool—the Church—that would, in turn, develop tools—disciples—to proclaim the gospel to every corner of the world. It is through the Church that disciples are formed who, in turn, create more disciples.

Unfortunately, many have become mere consumers of the Christian culture rather than committed disciples. "Church hopping" has become common. Now, you can church hop without ever leaving home, as many have exchanged face-to-face church community for an online experience. I'm not against podcasts or live stream services; we have them, and they are a great option for when you're traveling or home sick. It can never replace, though, the sweet fellowship we are made to receive from being together. Hebrews 10:24-25 says, *And let us consider how to stir up one another to love and good works, not neglecting to meet together, as is the habit of some, but encouraging one another, and all the more as you see the Day drawing near.* We need each other. When I was sick, I needed to see people serving God who had been healed. When I was in grief, I needed that prayer partner who prayed with me until God restored my joy. And when I've needed to grow up, I've needed people who saw things in my life and who addressed those things, as a loving, spiritual family member would—so that I wasn't stunted and unable to fulfill the destiny for my life.

Sometimes, I see people come to church, drawn there because of a crisis or need for the Lord's intervention in their lives. They're so excited at first, then as God works, and things get better, the new wears off and people think they can do it on their own. They lose the awe for the house of God, and the family that God intends to support us throughout our lives. They sometimes lose their hunger for God. It reminds me of when a new restaurant opens in Austin. For the first six months, you can't get in without a two-hour wait. But when the newness wears off and another new restaurant opens nearby, the crowds shift their allegiance. It's the same with churches in the United States. Someone starts a new church (which in itself is an excellent thing) with an exciting worship team (again, a very good thing), and people leave the church they've been attending to go to the new place or, sadly, sometimes they just leave church altogether.

I don't see these people as disciples, but as consumers. You will never become a disciple who can make other disciples unless you are like the tree described in the Psalms:

They are like trees along a riverbank bearing luscious fruit each season without fail. Their leaves shall never wither, and all they do shall prosper (Psalm 1:3 TLB).

Trees that are planted, then dug up and replanted over and over, have very little chance of survival, let alone producing fruit. In the same way, a Christian who church hops won't have strong roots needed to survive in hard times and to bear the fruit of the Spirit in their life. I am a fifth-generation minister. Being a committed member of a church is as natural to me as breathing. I call it being "planted in the house." To have a community of fellow disciples is an invaluable tool for all Christians, and especially for Christian leaders.

2. Scripture

Words are very important to God. In the beginning, God spoke, and things came to be. God spoke to His people, Israel, through the words He gave to the prophets. And of course, Jesus is the Word made flesh, the Word who dwelt among us. (See John 1:14.) We use words to convey thoughts, emotions, ideas, wisdom, hurts, encouragement. Words are what reveal our souls; words are what make us human.

And words are how God chooses to communicate with you and me today. He has given—through prophets, poets, historians, kings, biographers, preachers, and apostles—a collection of written material that has been gathered together, put in a specific order (called a "canon"), and passed down through the centuries called the Bible. In its words, we come to know our God in a very personal way. It isn't just a bullet-pointed list of things we are to do and not to do. The Bible, by using words, is a conversation between the Lord and us. An ongoing heart-to-heart with our loving Father, His Son our Savior, and the Holy Spirit.

It is given to us as a way to know God and communicate with Him, yes, but it is also a tool we are to carry with us at all times. It is a sword to use against the enemy (Ephesians 6:17) and, when used by someone with great skill, is a scalpel that can cut deep and accurately enough to divide between the soul and the spirit (Hebrews 4:12). The Word of God is the very life of God in us that causes us to be born again to an unending life (1 Peter 1:23). It is milk that nourishes (1 Peter 2:2). The Bible is a lamp to light the way we are to go (Psalm 119:105). It is a fire that consumes and a hammer that shatters (Jeremiah 23:29). The Bible is the Swiss Army knife of tools for the Christian leader.

3. Availability

Being available is often better than being proficient. The more you make yourself available, the more you will learn. The more you learn, the greater the responsibility you will receive. It is by first making yourself available that you begin to grow into leadership. It's not really complicated, but it is hard. It's hard to let go of your own wants and desires and say, "Yes, I can do that." Leaders in training make self-sacrifice a daily discipline until it becomes second nature.

Availability doesn't just mean clearing our calendars to accept a job or task. It also means to clear our expectations and agendas and accept what the Lord brings our way each day. We see this in the book of Acts where a great many people were coming to know the Lord. The gospel message was spreading from Jerusalem to Samaria and all the towns in between. The apostles were going from town to town, praying for the converts to receive the Holy Spirit. Signs and miracles were abundant. Why would anyone want to leave a great revival when it was at its peak? Yet that is what the Lord called Philip to do. Philip could have said, "No way I'm leaving this great event! This is where the action is—this is where the Spirit is moving." Philip could have done this, but instead, he made himself available to God's leading. And where was he led? Down a dirt road and into the desert—hardly the direction he (or we) would have chosen on our own. As he walked on this lonely road, he saw up ahead a man riding in a chariot. At God's urging, Philip ran up alongside the chariot and heard the man reading from the book of Isaiah, a passage that told of the coming Messiah.

"Do you understand what you're reading?" asked Philip.

"How can I unless someone teaches me?" replied the man. He then invited Philip to join him in his chariot. Again, Philip made himself available to the leading of the Spirit and got in with the man.

"Tell me," said the man to Philip, "who is being talked about here? Is the prophet himself or someone else?" And starting with that passage, Philip began to tell the man about Jesus. He must have shared the good news clearly and concisely, for as they approached a pond, the man said, "Look—there's some water. Will you baptize me?" And Philip, sensing that this was all going according to God's plan, baptized him right there.

Through Philip's obedience to the Lord and making himself available to God, the Lord used him in a significant way. This man in the chariot was very influential in the queen of Ethiopia's court. Through his influence, the good news of Jesus was spread in his country and all throughout Africa. Philip left one revival and, using the tool of availability, started another.

4. Accountability

Everyone wants to be a leader. Very few, however, are prepared to accept the accountability that goes with it. But you can't be a leader—at least, a godly, effective leader—without accepting responsibility for who and what you lead. You must be accountable for what you say you will do.

Just what does accountability in leadership mean?

Accountability means that you accept responsibility for the outcomes that come under your leadership—both good and bad. You don't blame others. And you don't blame the external conditions. Accountable leaders recognize there are always things they could have done—or still can do—to change the outcome.

Until you take responsibility, you are a victim of the actions of others and of the environment you are in. Being a victim is the opposite of being a leader. Victims are passive. They are acted upon. Leaders are active. They do what it takes to accomplish what they have committed to do.

Accountability is seen when people faithfully deliver on their commitments, showing others they can be trusted to do what they say they'll do. Leaders take responsibility for the outcomes of their actions and decisions, as well as those on their team. As famed leadership author Phil Geldart says in his book, *In Your Hands: The Behaviors of a World-Class Leader,* "Let the quality of your work and decisions be the gold standard against which the performance of others comes to be measured."

"Gold standard" accountability is of such a high quality that others see it as the best possible combination of talk and action, causing others to follow. It consists of excellent performance and the mastery of the key skills and behaviors necessary for a specific job. Here are some ways to build a "gold standard" accountability into your leadership.

- *Lead by Example*

  When you demonstrate accountability in your actions, you are setting the standard for excellence. You're also showing others how to be responsible for doing what they say they'll do. Accountable leaders exhibit:

- Discipline—they tend to the important rather than get distracted by the urgent
- Integrity—being honest about the likelihood of delivering on commitments, and accepting the blame when something goes wrong
- Execution—mastering new skills and behaviors to always accomplish tasks regardless of challenges that come their way

♦ *Develop Accountable Leaders*

You will want to encourage those just developing their leadership "wings" to practice accountability at all times. By building accountability into your leadership development program, they will learn how to deliver on commitments and see the importance of being reliable and trustworthy in the eyes of others.

♦ *Build Individual Understanding*

At the beginning of any project, individuals must understand expectations, what resources and support are available, and what they need to do to be accountable for their part. This helps to avoid the pitfall of over-committing and under-delivering. Some of the tools that can help support individual understanding of the need to be accountable include mentoring, monitoring, and meeting. As a mentor, you come alongside one or more of your team members to show them how to develop the skills she'll need to do her job well. In this way, you are more of a friend than a boss. And yet you'll need to monitor her work to be sure she is doing it correctly and in a timely manner. To accomplish this, regular meetings must be scheduled to see how she is doing and to help stretch her beyond her comfort zone.

5. Active

One more tool in a leader's tool belt—and one that is very easily left out—is to be active. What I mean by "active" is not to merely desire to work for the Lord as a leader, not just waiting for an opportunity to come your way. Lead by doing what lies at hand right now.

In 1998, the Lord led us to a new assignment. After five years of senior pastoring in a small community, we moved to Baton Rouge, Louisiana, where we'd attended college. Joe was offered a position as co-pastor of a large, long-established church that also had a big Christian school. There were more people in that church and school than we had in our whole town, and I wondered how I would be able to get to know people and be able to minister. I also had two small children, and after coming through a difficult, and very busy season, I wanted to take a break from working full time, so I took the best position they had available, part-time receptionist, which also happened to be school nurse. I got really good at bandaging knee scrapes, hosting walk-in guests, and handling multiple calls for the school and church, all at the same time. The funniest day was when I was bandaging a child's knee and answering a phone call when a bee stung my finger. I never missed a beat!

Most people would consider this position a demotion from my previous jobs and responsibilities, but it was just where I needed to be to meet people and to minister to their needs. A year into my receptionist job, I was offered a position as a public relations director of one of the largest cancer treatment centers in the South. As a former cancer patient myself, I was excited about this opportunity and the benefits that came with it. When I went to resign from my receptionist position and to tell our senior pastor about my new opportunity, he was puzzled. "Let me see your resume," he said. After looking it over, he said, "Why didn't you tell me you had this kind of experience? I want you to be the public relations director for our school. I can't

WHEN YOU DON'T HESITATE AT "SMALL BEGINNINGS," GOD CAN OPEN BIG DOORS.

pay you more than the cancer center but I can give you a teacher's schedule, holidays and summers off."

Ambition didn't open that door for me. God did. All I did was to step into the door that was opened—even though it wasn't a fancy door! Most opportunities will come to you in seed form. I think we sometimes miss God (seed) opportunities, waiting on perfect (fully bloomed) opportunities. Because I didn't hesitate at a "small beginning," God opened a big door. God will never waste your gift, but as we faithfully serve and steward what He's entrusted to us, He will, at the right time, open the right doors. Proverbs 18:16 says, *"A man's gift makes room for him and brings him before the great."*

We see the tool of activity in what Jesus told His disciples as He compared the land of Israel to a field of grain.

"And Jesus went throughout all the cities and villages, teaching in their synagogues and proclaiming the gospel of the kingdom and healing every disease and every affliction. When he saw the crowds, he had compassion for them, because they were harassed and helpless, like sheep without a shepherd. Then he said to his disciples, 'The harvest is plentiful, but the laborers are few; therefore pray earnestly to the Lord of the harvest to send out laborers into his harvest'" (Matthew 9:35-38).

Notice Jesus did not say, "Pray for those willing to be laborers," or "Pray for those willing to give it a try." He said to ask the disciples to pray for *laborers* to be sent into the fields to harvest souls. A laborer is one who is already working, already active in some way. Just as there is a law of physics that says a body at rest remains at rest, we also learn that a body in motion tends to stay in motion. The Lord wants those who are already in motion, no matter what direction you are moving. The Apostle Paul was chosen to preach the gospel to Gentiles while he was in motion, even though he was moving in the opposite direction. Paul was seeking out Christians and dragging them before the Jewish religious leaders to be tortured or killed. God saw him in motion and, with a firm "tap," sent him in the right direction—into the fields ripe for harvest. The rest of your tool belt is meaningless if you don't get up and move.

Before you go anywhere, be sure you have your tool belt buckled and ready. The fields Jesus mentioned? They are still ripe for the harvest.

CHAPTER 12

LEAD UP

A new commandment I give to you, that you love one another: just as I have loved you, you also are to love one another.

John 13:34

"If your actions create a legacy that inspires others to dream more, learn more, do more and become more, then you are an excellent leader."

—Dolly Parton

You have made it to the final chapter, which tells me you are one of two people—either a woman who knows she is called by God to be a leader, or my mom. Assuming you are not my mom, you are a woman desiring to grow in your role as a leader, to walk more fully in your calling. You are not content to be merely an adequate leader. You desire to give your all for the glory of God. In this last chapter, I want to share some very straightforward, practical ideas you can incorporate in your life so that you are always growing toward greatness as a leader.

Let me first say this clearly: As Christians, we will be held account-able for how we loved here on earth. Leaders are not exempt from this. As a matter of fact, we read in James 3:1 (GNT), *My friends, not many of you should become teachers. As you know, we teachers will be judged with greater strictness than others.* Substitute "leaders" for "teachers" (for what is a teacher but a leader of those seeking knowl-edge and wisdom?) and we read a grave warning. Leaders will be held to a higher standard, and we will be measured by how we love others. The greatest leaders love others the way Jesus loves us—uncondition-ally, extravagantly, sacrificially. You cannot be a great leader without great love. And loving greatly only comes as we submit our lives to the Lord in obedience to Scripture.

Believe me, becoming a great leader is very hard work. Only a few are willing to put forth the continuous effort it takes to become a remarkable leader. And it would be better not to pursue leadership if you don't count the cost ahead of time. Being a mediocre leader is not only destructive for your own soul, but for those who follow you as well. Mediocrity creates more mediocrity. Settling for average from ourselves and others comes from sloth, lack of confidence, and apathy. And none of these attitudes are worthy of the Spirit of God who lives within us.

Do you find it hard to hear that being the leader God wants you to be entails hard work? Somehow, we have become a culture that avoids hardship at all costs. We not only run from suffering; we won't even put up with inconvenience. Our grandparents and great-grand-parents lived through the Great Depression, working twelve hours a day, six days a week, just to survive. Hard work and self-sacrifice came naturally to them. When our nation was attacked by Japan and threatened by Germany, signaling our entry into World War II, men everywhere gave up their families, homes, and financial security to join the military to fight for freedom and justice. Boys, including my grandfather, would lie about their age just to enlist and do what they saw as their duty. They are now referred to as the Greatest Generation for their sacrifice and perseverance in the face of incredible challenges.

At the same time, we saw a surge in the numbers of men and women who left all and became missionaries, spreading the good news of Jesus around the world. These missionaries started hospitals and schools, introduced first-world medical practices into third-world nations. They, just like soldiers in the military, fought for freedom and justice—freedom from the deadly consequences of sin and justice for those oppressed by the tyranny of Satan.

Where are these courageous men and women today? The number of those enlisting in the armed forces has declined to where it is difficult to defend against all of the threats we face today. And the same with missionaries. Their numbers have declined precipitously in the last decade. Why is this?

I'm sure many who are experts in their fields can cite social, economic, educational, and political reasons for the declines in both the military and mission organizations. But I see another reason, one that lies at the foot of churches in our day. I call this the deception of easy discipleship.

COUNTING THE COST

Jesus was walking toward Jerusalem, knowing that once He arrived there He would be crucified. Large crowds followed Him, some simply on their way to celebrate the Passover at the Temple, but many others listening to Jesus teach about living life in the Kingdom of God. We read in Luke's Gospel what Jesus spoke to these people.

One day when large groups of people were walking along with him, Jesus turned and told them,

"Anyone who comes to me but refuses to let go of father, mother, spouse, children, brothers, sisters—yes, even one's own self!—can't

be my disciple. Anyone who won't shoulder his own cross and follow behind me can't be my disciple.

"Is there anyone here who, planning to build a new house, doesn't first sit down and figure the cost so you'll know if you can complete it? If you only get the foundation laid and then run out of money, you're going to look pretty foolish. Everyone passing by will poke fun at you: 'He started something he couldn't finish.'

"Or can you imagine a king going into battle against another king without first deciding whether it is possible with his ten thousand troops to face the twenty thousand troops of the other? And if he decides he can't, won't he send an emissary and work out a truce?

"Simply put, if you're not willing to take what is dearest to you, whether plans or people, and kiss it good-bye, you can't be my disciple" (Luke 14:25-33 MSG).

There are no surprises for those who want to follow Jesus—it will cost you everything. Everything. Carrying a cross is not a fashion statement. When Jesus spoke those words to the crowd, they knew exactly what He meant. Only those about to suffer torture and death at the hands of the Romans carried crosses. They would soon see Jesus Himself nailed to a cross. The words spoken by the Lord just days before—"shoulder your own cross"—came home in a very real and terrible way. In order to follow Jesus, we must let go of everything and embrace, rather than run from, suffering.

But Jesus did not leave us without consolation. *"I have said these things to you, that in me you may have peace. In the world you will have tribulation. But take heart; I have overcome the world"* (John 16:33). No promises of an easy life, only the promise that He will always be with us and, as we trust more and more in Him, we will have peace in the midst of the storms of life.

Just don't think we can take the easy road and still pursue holiness. Mother Angelica, a Catholic nun and the founder of one of the largest Christian media networks in the world, said, "Holiness is not for wimps, and the Cross is not negotiable, sweetheart—it's a requirement." C. S. Lewis also wrote about this in his classic, *Mere Christianity*. "If you want a religion to make you feel really comfortable, I certainly don't recommend Christianity."

LEADERSHIP IS NOT FOR WIMPS

Many start down the "Jesus road," but soon get distracted by the things of this world. There has been no counting of the cost, no true commitment to following Jesus in the good times and bad.

"Christianity has not been tried and found wanting," wrote G. K. Chesterton, "it has been found difficult and not tried."

Being a Christian leader is even harder. It is certainly not for wimps. Focusing on leading others to a more intimate relationship with the Lord means forsaking the good things of this world—family time, financial success, status, getting to do your own thing—so you can give of yourself to others. The tug of this world's way of doing things is very strong. It takes great perseverance and trust in the Lord to keep on the narrow road that leads to life. Over the past few years, I've noticed, and so have many of my ministry-leading peers, an uptick in young people leaving ministry positions at our churches. They aren't leaving because they've had a bad experience. In fact, many stay connected to the church. They crave comfort. They want weekends off. For many, once they have children, they make their little ones their call instead of modeling to them how to follow the call of God even if that means we have to make sacrifices. They failed to count the cost that comes with the call to be leaders in the Kingdom. As I previously admitted, my work-life balance hasn't always been in balance. If "too much church" drives kids out of church, my "PKs" (preacher's kids) should hate church, and as a PK myself, so should I. But that's not the case. There are no church haters in my crew. In fact, my adult kids attend and serve every time the doors are open, and they take vacation time off to go to church conferences.

I want you to hear me loud and clear on this. I have recently become an empty nester after more than two and a half decades of having children under my roof. Had I waited to follow the call of God for my life (whether that be in vocational ministry, in the marketplace, or in the community), I would have missed the peak time of my life to follow God's calling. More importantly, my kids would have missed out on the ride of their lives, being a part of a family who gives it all for God. A family who risks, who sacrifices, and who says, "Yes!" And because we said, "Yes!" our kids are saying "Yes" to their calls. They are risking, sacrificing, and giving it a go. We aren't called to play it safe. If you're a mom, you aren't called to center your life around your children, but we are all called to center our lives and our families around the King.

In *The Message,* Jesus' call to come to Him when we are weary and need rest (Matthew 11:28-30) reads like this. *"Are you tired? Worn out? Burned out on religion? Come to me. Get away with me and you'll recover your life. I'll show you how to take a real rest. Walk with me and work with me—watch how I do it. Learn the unforced rhythms of grace. I won't lay anything heavy or ill-fitting on you. Keep company with me and you'll learn to live freely and lightly."*

Please don't misunderstand me. When the Lord asks us if we have what it takes to stay with Him, the only correct answer is, "No, Lord, I don't." There is no one who can obey the call to *"be perfect, as your heavenly Father is perfect"* (Matthew 5:48) on their own. We cannot please God in our own power. We must see that we are spiritually poor, empty of what it takes to walk the path Jesus walked—to His death—before we can then be filled with the Holy Spirit. It is God's Spirit living in us who enables us to go through hard times with peace. Our job is to remain surrendered to the Holy Spirit at all times.

Years ago, we were at a pastors' conference and met some leaders of the underground, persecuted church, and we asked them what their takeaways were from their visit to America. They said, "We are surprised at how much the American church is able to do without much prayer." Ouch! It was one of those "humbly offensive" statements. With all of our conveniences, it's possible to settle for a successful life when we can have a supernatural one.

YOU WEREN'T MADE FOR THE MUNDANE; YOU WERE MADE FOR THE MIRACULOUS!

MADE FOR THE MIRACULOUS

It's easy to slip into mundane when we're made for the miraculous. This thought came to me so strongly recently as I was having one of those mindless mornings, scrolling through Facebook, as I tried to wake up. A young woman's post popped up on my feed—not just any young woman, but one whose life is a total miracle. About thirty-five years ago, when I was a teenager, in my home church, a young married couple announced they were expecting a child. Four months into the pregnancy, the doctors gave the wife/mom the terrible news that she had stage four cancer. They advised the couple to abort the baby to begin aggressive treatment. Our whole church went to prayer. The couple decided to believe for a miracle, and to proceed with cancer treatment but to not abort. Each time the mom went for chemotherapy, the doctors would warn that the baby in her womb would surely not survive, and if the child did survive, she would be terribly malformed and mentally challenged. During that time, we had a couple of guest speakers come through our church that called this couple out, without any knowledge of what she was going through, and prophesied life over her and her baby. The Lord gave my mom a prophetic verse for her as well, that God was shielding the child from the effects of the cancer treatment.

I'll never forget the phone call we got that this healthy baby girl was born, and how she had a head full of hair (in spite of all the chemo treatments). We rushed to the hospital where we filled the waiting room with celebration, crying happy tears and rejoicing that our Great Physician had shown up in such a powerful way. Our whole church had witnessed nothing less than a miracle! Not a thing was wrong with this child—she was perfect and intelligent in every way, and her mom was healed in the process too.

You just imagine that with that kind of miracle, that this child is going to grow up to be one of the greatest evangelists of the 21st century. My curiosity got the best of me and I did some Facebook "research" (aka spying) which led me to a different conclusion. She's grown up now, and is a working mom, beautiful and healthy. What was absent from mention is any relationship at all with the Lord. I was looking at her life and her lifestyle through images and comments, thinking, "Don't you know you're a miracle? Don't you know how many around-the-clock prayers were prayed that you would live? Don't you know you're made for so much more than the life you're living?"

Girl, you are not living like you're a miracle. Honestly, I rolled that around in my head for several days, burdened about it, wondering if I should reach out and remind her of her story—but she hasn't seen me since she was a child and would probably think I'm crazy and meddling. Then, I started thinking, "How many of us are not living like miracles?" Jesus went to great lengths for you to know Him. Maybe you don't have as dramatic a story as she does, but there's a story in your life. I think when we're in Heaven, we're going to find out the many times that God miraculously saved our lives when we didn't even know it.

You are a miracle. Make the most of it. You are called to live a redeemed life. Every single thing that was meant to destroy you should be a weapon to free others. Every gift we have, be it our voice, our strong will, our wisdom, our experiences, or our leadership, aren't for our own pleasure but for His glory.

Your gifts aren't made to be hoarded. Your experiences are made to encourage others. The miracle of this very family is the one that cheered me on when I was going through cancer while pregnant. We all need someone to look to who went before us in the same battle and got the victory. That's leadership.

There are no shortcuts to holiness. And there are no shortcuts to being the leader God is calling you to be. Leadership also isn't one victory after another. You are going to have many failures—as well as successes—as you begin to Woman Up and take on leadership duties. But do not let either failure or success define who you are. Don't let circumstances change who God has made you to be. His plans for your life may not be the same as for others, but we know they are plans for our good. God's plans for you are for prosperity and protection; for hope and a future. (See Jeremiah 29:11.) Stay surrendered to the Lord and trust in His ways at all times. And when you wander away from where He has placed you, know that He is quick to forgive and to restore you in gentleness to where you need to be.

Woman Up!

LETTER TO MY FUTURE SELF

Years ago, I realized that had I written a vision for my life, what God has already done would have surpassed everything I could ever have imagined. However, since I began this book with a letter to my younger self, I challenged myself to imagine what my future may look like, having grown in courage, surrounding myself with inspiring relationships, and planting myself in the purpose of God and His family. Here is my letter to my future self. I challenge you, as the reader, to do the same thing, as we all choose to Woman Up!

Dear Future Lori,

Imagine what your life would have been had you not stepped out of your comfort and into your calling. Maybe safer. Maybe calmer. Maybe more balanced.

How boring.

You were not made for boring. You were not even made to get the perfect amount of beauty rest, so that you literally step up to the pearly gates "without wrinkle or blemish."

Nope, you were made to leave it all on the field. You work on Earth and rest in Heaven (while not forsaking the occasional Sabbath, of course). The work the Lord has given you has been so vital, from the seasons of diaper changing and bedtime stories to the seasons of church planting, and campus expansions; and, of course, the season through it all being a wife, while always remaining a girlfriend to Joe.

The fruit of your obedience is countless. Many have watched you Woman Up, and in seeing you they got the courage to do so, too. You didn't always make it look easy—you were transparent in your struggles and insecurities, but that actually emboldened others to say, "If she can do it, so can I." And you delight in those stories.

Early in your marriage, Joe asked you how you wanted to be marked as a leader, and you said, "I want to raise up people who go so much further than we could ever go. Better communicators. Better pastors. Better leaders. People whose floor is our ceiling. I want to just watch them go." And God has answered the desire of your heart. In fact, He answered it because He placed it there to begin with.

And your children, the ones who were enlisted into this life without their permission, are so much better for it. They are strong men equipped to stand in their convictions. Men of God who married equally strong women and are together leading their families in the ways of the Lord.

You don't feel it's necessary to lie about your age, because you couldn't be paid enough to do twenty-nine again. You've earned every fine line and wrinkle, and through victories and challenges, you've placed your trust in an unshakeable God. The mark of a Woman Up woman is that she keeps exiting her comfort zone and saying "Yes!" to God. And this is what you are meant to do for the rest of your life.

Keep on and Woman Up, Lori!

WOMAN UP: DISCUSSION QUESTIONS

EXERCISE: *Just like Lori has done in the beginning of the book, begin with writing a letter to your younger self. Think about a time in your life when it would have been significant to write yourself a letter of encouragement to keep you going on the journey.*

Chapter 1:

1. Thinking back upon your childhood, would you describe yourself as more of a leader or a follower? Why or why not?

2. What, if anything, do you think disqualifies you from leadership?

3. God is calling each of us to make a difference within our sphere of influence and many of us do not realize the scope and magnitude of that sphere. Take a moment to make a list of who you interact with on a regular basis (the cashier at your local coffee shop, the receptionist at the school, your hairdresser, your small group, etc.) This is your sphere!

Chapter 2:

1. Lori shared about a painful defining moment in her life regarding the death of her father. Reflecting on your own life, are there defining moments of where you felt (or did not feel) the presence of God near or feared that you would never again?

2. Lori reminded us that "Some 'Deborah's' aren't women ... they are people—men and women—who cause you to stop shrinking (physically and emotionally) and stand tall. They celebrate your uniqueness." Thinking upon your own life, who are your "Deborah's," past or present? Why?

3. What are ways that you can encourage and strengthen another within those you know? How can you go about putting that into action?

Chapter 3:

1. Lori challenges us with thoughts regarding our past. We can live amazing lives for God even with the darkest past, or we can live our past as the only life we know. Which would others describe you living? How can you begin to lay aside the past and start to run the race God has called you to?

2. What area of your life are you struggling to "get back up" from? What are the obstacles that keep you from starting over?

3. Reflect on a "down season" where you may have had to faith it over faking it until you reached your "up season." Now is a great time to remind yourself that you have courage and faith in difficult circumstances! Write this memory on a note card to pull out as a reminder when you need it.

Chapter 4:

1. Do you consider yourself to be a courageous person? Why or why not?

2. What fears do you hold that may keep you from walking in boldness in your calling?

3. When you go through difficult seasons, trials, and battles what insecurities within yourself do you recognize the most? Has this kept you frozen from moving forward?

4. What "buts" do you offer up the most when people try to call you out of your comfort zone?

Chapter 5:

1. Think outside the box. What are some ways you can live to make a difference in the life of God's people? Think back to those you listed in your sphere of influence in Chapter 1.

2. What are some areas of life you are blending in when you should be standing out?

3. Where is your passion level for God right now? For church? For the Body of Christ?

4. As believers, we all have experienced the passion and filling of the Lord's presence in our lives. And if we have walked with Christ long enough, we have also experienced valleys where we have forgotten how it feels to experience that presence. If we continue to show up, Lori reminds us that we too, will once again welcome that presence. Take a moment to think about a time when you may have felt this emptiness and write it here.

Chapter 6:

1. Have you let previous failures and/or a fear of failing again keep you from moving forward or trying something new? If so, commit to being bold and courageous in obedience to what God has asked you to do.

2. When in life have you felt spiritual gravity holding you down?

3. What are some ways you can improve your attitude within your circumstances? Commit to being a leader of hope rather than a purveyor of despair.

Chapter 7:

1. What has been your impression of the Proverbs 31 woman?

2. Who has God placed in your care? How are you working to protect them today?

3. As women, we carry the roles of protector, being multifaceted and uncomplicated, being strategic, secure, and inspirational. Thinking over each of these descriptions, which area could use more consistency and intentionality within your leadership? How can you develop that?

Chapter 8:

1. As a leader, you are aware of your strengths. Oftentimes, the Lord pairs us with people (men or women) who are different than us. In what ways could they benefit from your weaknesses?

2. Have you ever tried to be someone you were not? What qualities or characteristics were you striving to emulate?

3. What would it take for you to know it was "okay to lead with strength"? List these out. You may be surprised to find you may have already put some of these into action.

Chapter 9:

1. How would you describe a person who has true humility?

2. How do you ensure you are walking in humility in your own life, being both realistic about your shortcomings, yet confident in who you are and your giftings?

3. Have you encountered a humble leader in life that you respect and admire? How did they treat other people and make others feel?

4. Are you able to recognize others' worth and talents, yes or no? Are you also able to recognize your own? If you are, use this space to write them down. If you are not, explain why.

Chapter 10:

1. Are you purposeful in building a team atmosphere around you? In what ways?

2. In what ways can you personally improve how you communicate in regard to your words, mannerisms, your emotions, and your presence?

3. Would you say you are more or less adaptable to change? List some ways that you are able to move forward, even if it's just the next step!

Chapter 11:

1. Lori lists five tools we should have to be effective leaders: Develop Disciples, Being Available, Being Accountable, Leading by Example, and to Be Active. Which of these would you say you are doing well? Which do you need to improve? How can you do that?

2. God has the ability to provide doors for opportunity for us. While God is aware of the big desires of your heart, He also has smaller seeds of opportunities for us. What are some ways that you can continue to faithfully serve and steward what God has entrusted to you now, before the big opportunity has arrived?

Chapter 12:

1. Describe some difficulties you may have encountered in choosing to follow Jesus.

2. Are you hoarding your gifts? Are you hoarding your testimony? What ways can you help free others by the miraculous that God has done in your life?

EXERCISE: *Just like Lori has done at the end of the book, write a letter to your future self as we all choose to Woman Up!*

WOMAN UP: ENCOURAGING STATEMENTS

God did not create you to be anyone's doormat, and that includes your own. God is calling you to WOMAN UP from fear, shame, and insecurity.

When you feel like you are up against 900 chariots, remember that obedience always wins.

Real strength is continuing to get up, even when nothing in you feels like going on.

Great leaders inspire courage and greatness in others.

Look beyond people's POSITION and see their POTENTIAL.

Sometimes your problems will seem bigger than God's promise.

We've got to give up to go up.

Never compromise God's call for your comfort.

It's not *faking* it, it's *faithing* it! Leaders give up the right to completely fall apart every time they feel like it.

GO UP, and call others to come up WITH YOU.

Never let fear keep you from being the leader God has called you to be. The enemy will use fear to keep you tied to the dock instead of sailing in the ocean of God's grace.

You lack nothing when the Spirit of God is with you.

God's command + our obedience = the miraculous.

Do not worry about fitting in when you are supposed to stand out.

Showing up will wake you up.

GAIN GROUND as you push past the gravity trying to keep you down. Anti-gravity leaders are both ALTITUDE and ATTITUDE shifters.

God made woman as a solution to the problem of ALONENESS.

Her PROTECTOR became her ACCUSER.

We aren't to lead at the expense of men, but alongside them.

It's not about competition, it's about completion.

Speak to potential, not to posture.

Some women are not facing a glass ceiling, but a FEELINGS CEILING.

Learn to accept criticism and deflect praise.

Leaders aren't made in GREENROOMS or BOARDROOMS, but the best leaders are in touch with REAL PEOPLE.

If you aren't TEACHABLE, you aren't TEAMABLE.

STRONG LEADERS have the STRENGTH OF HUMILITY.

Communication is the food of leadership.

Your purpose is not your title.

When you don't hesitate at "small beginnings," God can open BIG DOORS.

You weren't made for the mundane; you were made for the miraculous!

AUTHOR CONTACT

If you would like to contact Lori Champion, find out more information, purchase books, or request her to speak, please contact:

lorichampion.com

Celebration Church
601 Westinghouse Road
Georgetown, TX 78626
512.763.3000

Follow Lori!
twitter.com/lorimchampion
instagram.com/lorimchampion